The Psychology of Success

Prentice Hall LIFE

If life is what you make it, then making it better starts here.

What we learn today can change our lives tomorrow. It can change our goals or change our minds; open up new opportunities or simply inspire us to make a difference. That's why we have created a new breed of books that do more to help you make more of *your* life.

Whether you want more confidence or less stress, a new skill or a different perspective, we've designed *Prentice Hall Life* books to help you to make a change for the better. Together with our authors we share a commitment to bring you the brightest ideas and best ways to manage your life, work and wealth.

In these pages we hope you'll find the ideas you need for the life *you* want. Go on, help yourself.

It's what you make it

* * *

The Psychology of Success

Secrets of serial achievement

Judith Leary-Joyce

Harlow, England • London • New York • Boston • San Francisco • Toronto • Sydney • Singapore • Hong Kong
Tokyo • Seoul • Taipei • New Delhi • Cape Town • Madrid • Mexico City • Amsterdam • Munich • Paris • Milan

PEARSON EDUCATION LIMITED

Edinburgh Gate
Harlow CM20 2JE
Tel: +44 (0)1279 623623
Fax: +44 (0)1279 431059
Website: www.pearsoned.co.uk

First published in Great Britain in 2009

ISBN: 978-0-273-72089-8

British Library Cataloguing-in-Publication Data
A catalogue record for this book is available from the British Library

Library of Congress Cataloging-in-Publication Data
Leary-Joyce, Judith.
    The psychology of success : secrets of serial achievement / Judith Leary-Joyce.
        p. cm
    Includes index.
    ISBN 978-0-273-72089-8 (pbk.)
    1. Success--Psychological aspects. 2. Success in business. I. Title.
    BF637.S8L422 2009
    158--dc22
                                        2009014820

10 9 8 7 6 5 4 3 2 1
13 12 11 10 09

Typeset in 10pt IowanOldStyle by 3
Printed and bound in Great Britain by Henry Ling Ltd, Dorchester, Dorset

The publisher's policy is to use paper manufactured from sustainable forests.

This book is dedicated to you and your success.

Use your core talent and make the very best of your life: then you too will look back on a life well used.

"As a well spent day brings happy sleep, so a life well used brings happy death"

Leonardo da Vinci

Contents

About the author

JUDITH LEARY-JOYCE is a serial achiever with a number of careers under her belt. She spent twenty years as a Gestalt Psychotherapist and managing director of a major training centre in London.

She then moved into business consultancy, working globally with senior leaders and managers. In 2002, she established Great Companies Consulting, bringing together a team of experts to help public and private organisations become more productive places to work. This expertise informed her first book, *Becoming an Employer of Choice*.

In 2004, she wrote *Inspirational Manager*, inspiring many middle and senior managers to review their style and team working, leading to improved business results.

The Psychology of Success brings together a lifetime of learning, including teacher, social worker, mother, grandmother, business consultant and speaker. The route map she has created will enable you to contribute your best to our fast moving global community – and enjoy yourself along the way!

Contact Judith with your comments, questions and stories by logging on to **www.thepsychologyofsuccess.co.uk** or **www.judithlearyjoyce.com**.

About the contributors

Jim Al-Khalili OBE

Jim Al-Khalili is a professor of physics at the University of Surrey and holds a chair in the public engagement in science.

He has written several popular science books and regularly contributes to science and history programmes on both radio and television. He is currently writing a book on medieval Arabic science.

In 2007, he received the Royal Society's Michael Faraday medal and prize and his picture is part of the National Portrait Gallery's 21 Faces of British Science exhibition.

Jim is vice-president of the British Science Association and a senior adviser to the British Council.

Tunde Banjoko

Tunde is the chief executive of Local Employment Access Projects (LEAP) and his early story is similar to those of many young people who get caught up with trying to 'fit in' on the streets of the UK's inner cities. He is now chief executive of a charity that has successfully transformed the lives of thousands of people from disadvantaged communities, by empowering them with the confidence and attitude to provide for themselves and their families. He sits on a number of governmental advisory bodies, gives presentations on a London Business School leadership programme and was awarded an OBE in 2008.

Website: **www.leap.org.uk**.

Mark Barnard

Mark Barnard held several jobs in design and project management before spotting an opportunity to 'have a go' at his own business. He believes recognising the niche and having a supportive family were crucial to success. Contrasol is now in year three of trading, continuously expanding and offering a service that exceeds customer satisfaction. With careful management and a hands-on approach, the company's future looks exciting.

With all the effort and time a new business takes, Mark is keen to remember to enjoy his family as well as the fruits of the business: 'You're not here long!'

Website: **www.contrasol.com**.

Jill Black

Jill is a garden designer and landscaper who won a silver medal at the Chelsea Flower Show. She started out as a teacher but marriage to an RAF pilot meant moving every three years. Teaching was not always an option, particularly once her children were born. Instead, she embarked on projects including a children's playgroup, a business designing and making children's clothes, teaching English as a foreign language, becoming an advisory teacher, studying to become a garden designer and running a holiday cottage. She lives in Hertfordshire with her husband and has three grandchildren.

Website: **www.olddrifthouse.co.uk**.

Susan Bull

Susan began her fashion career with designer Louis Feraud in London's West End. She opened her first shop aged twenty-one and three more before her daughter was born.

Having designed a collection of children's clothes and developed a career as a stylist and personal shopper, she was approached by a national department store to create a fashion advisory service. This covered twenty-eight stores and involved training staff, creating and presenting fashion shows and media appearances.

In 2004, Susan opened a boutique called SuSu in Welwyn, Hertfordshire, and recently joined with her daughter to open another store in Radlett.

Website: **www.susu-style.co.uk**.

Naaz Coker

Naaz Coker runs a management consultancy and is chair of St George's Healthcare NHS Trust. She spent twenty years in the NHS and ten at the King's Fund.

Naaz has chaired Shelter and the British Refugee Council. She is a trustee of the RSA and council member of St George's University.

Naaz grew up in Tanzania and achieved a degree, MSc and MBA in the UK.

She was named 'Asian Woman of the Year' twice and 'Asian Woman of Achievement' in the public sector.

She has been awarded honorary doctorate degrees by Leeds Metropolitan University and the University of Central England.

Gina Coleman

After failing her A-levels, Gina Coleman lost her place at a poly-technic and attended a secretarial course instead. With her ambition fired to progress as far as possible in her career without 'proper' qualifications, two secretarial jobs later she landed 'the most exciting and enjoyable job ever' working for a stockbroker in the City of London for nine years.

Internal promotion brought Gina a career that she loved – media relations – and culminated in her becoming head of media relations for an investment bank. Now 'retired', Gina is a fundraising volunteer and trustee at her local hospice.

Simon Duffy PhD FRSA

Simon is chief executive of In Control, a charity leading the reform of the welfare system to promote citizenship for all. Simon was a Harkness fellow in 1994. He is the founder of Inclusion Glasgow and Altrum. He is an honorary senior fellow at the University of Birmingham's health service management centre and has a doctorate in moral philosophy. In 2008, Simon was awarded the RSA's Prince Albert Medal for social innovation for his work in developing self-directed support. More information about Simon and his work is available at **www.simonduffy.info**.

Murray Dunlop

After graduating from the University of York with a degree in computer science, Murray has spent the last nine years working in the financial sector. Starting off in a technical role, he quickly progressed into project management, achieving the title of vice-president by the age of twenty-six. He has co-ordinated a variety of large information technology projects, including office migrations, data centre expansions and business start-ups. He now manages a group of project managers and has a strong track record of coaching staff and developing high-performing teams.

Barbara Evans

Barbara was born in Kent before moving to Cheshire with her family when she was eight years old. Barbara worked for Barclays Bank for nine years after leaving school before going to live in Sydney for three years. On her return from Australia, Barbara worked in various organisations before finally fulfilling a long-held ambition to become a police officer with Cheshire Constabulary at the age of forty-eight, a case of now or never.

Barbara was following in her maternal grandfather's footsteps as he was an inspector in the Flying Squad in the Metropolitan Police.

Craig Fazzini-Jones

Craig Fazzini-Jones is an executive director of Marine & General Mutual Life Assurance Society, heading up their specialist retirement business. He set up his first businesses aged fifteen, tired of working hard for the minimum wage. He moved from America to the UK to obtain a business degree, then worked for Procter & Gamble in sales. Craig became interested in financial services while working for Accenture and moved to HBOS where he led the UK's largest annuity broker, as well as holding other senior roles. He is married to Amanda, and is the proud father of two girls.

Contact: **rcraigjones@yahoo.co.uk**.

Dr Eversley Felix

Eversley is a senior learning and development consultant within the BBC and specialises in leadership development, project management, organisational change, action learning and building teams. He has worked in a variety of public and private sector organisations. He has a doctorate in business administration and an advanced diploma in organisational consulting from Henley Business School and Brunel University. He also has an advanced diploma in executive coaching from the Academy of Executive Coaching. He is a professional certified coach with the International Coaching Federation and an accredited professional executive coach with the Academy of Executive Coaching.

Contact: **eversley.felix@bbc.co.uk**.

Derek Ffoulkes

Derek Ffoulkes is married to Shirley and is passionate about his family. They have two grown-up sons, Nick and Rob; Nick is engaged to Karen.

Derek lists travel among the things he enjoys most and his favourite building is the Palazzo Vecchio in Florence. Also, he is enjoying the resurgence of Welsh rugby.

Derek is committed to lifelong learning and is an advocate of self-knowledge; he describes himself as a 'work in progress'.

Derek is head of human resources and organisational development with a group of housing associations in the North West of England.

Peter Fisher

Born in Lancashire, Peter Fisher failed his 11+ but completed A-levels and worked in retail management. He was a social worker from 1971 to 1980, with cared-for children, for the GLC child guidance service and as placements manager.

In 1980, he started a computer business, P&P plc. Although he took semi-retirement in 1985 to care for his young sons, he remained as chairman and then non-executive director. The company was listed on the London stock market in 1988.

He was a governor of his old school and chair of the Rossendale Local Strategic Partnership. He lives on the Isle of Man.

Paul Gayler

Paul Gayler discovered a passion for food aged twelve, assisting his mother with the family catering business.

He attended catering school and passed with the highest honours, then worked in some of Britain's finest restaurants and hotels.

In 1982, he left the Dorchester to become head chef at Inigo Jones where he gained an enviable reputation as a pioneer for haute vegetarian cuisine. In 1991, Paul was invited to head up the team of the newly opened Lanesborough Hotel on Hyde Park.

Paul lives in Essex, is married to Anita and they have four children.

Website: **www.paulgayler.com**.

Helen Hanson

Helen was born in the UK and has lived in New Zealand, worked in Europe and the US, and is now in Hong Kong with a young family.

A grade 8 clarinettist and accomplished jazz saxophonist, Helen is also a keen sportswoman excelling in competition for road and track cycling, tennis, cricket and running.

Her passion is the development and understanding of people and she has held influential learning and development roles in international companies. Currently she is self-employed and works on enabling lasting, positive developmental change with individuals and organisations.

She has an MIPD from the Institute of Personnel & Development, is a master NLP practitioner, time line therapist and hypnotist, has a certificate in management studies and post-graduate diploma in personnel management from Oxford Brookes University and a BA from Canterbury University.

Harriet Kelsall

Born in St Albans to a family of jewellers, architects and artists, Harriet Kelsall made her first ring aged four! She chose industrial design at Brunel University where she achieved a first class degree and won the university prize. From there, she forged a successful career in the computer industry before deciding to found her own company in 1998. Harriet Kelsall Jewellery Design has steadily grown to become one of the UK's leading bespoke jewellery design companies with an impressive collection of awards to its name and customers all over the world.

Website: **www.hkjewellery.co.uk.**

Su Lissanevitch

Su is an eco-builder living in Bulgaria. She specialises in designing and building earthen homes and wood-burning rocket stoves. In the past she was a teacher of English, a ceramicist, an international public speaker on many aspects of health and well-being and a tutor of complementary medicine, and an Ayurvedic practitioner. All of these skills and qualifications are useful in her present career. She is available as a consultant on the subject of earthern structures and homes. She hosts courses and mini holidays in Bulgaria for people interested in learning how to live a more carefree life.

Website: **www.ayurvedic-tours.co.uk.**

Zena Martin

Zena is the founder and managing director of Acknowledge Communications, a diversity communications and CSR consultancy that works with clients such as Sky, Kellogg's, the NHS and DWP. Zena's career spans twenty years of marketing communications in the US, Europe, Middle East and Africa, ranging from advertising to in-house marketing communications to public relations. Her experience hails from the likes of Leo Burnett, DDB Needham and McCann Erickson and UniWorld Group in advertising; BellSouth, in-house; and Text 100, Firefly Communications and Hill & Knowlton in public relations, where she was a managing director and board director.

Website: **www.acknowledgecommunications.com.**

Miriam McLoughlin

Miriam McLoughlin discovered a passion for theatre and performing at a young age. She has taken part in many shows, both on the stage performing and working behind the scenes with costume, make-up, lighting, stage management and assistant to the director. After completing A-levels at the Rudolf Steiner School, she pursued her passion for partner dancing, teaching salsa in Delhi and Mumbai. She also took part in a Bollywood film, *I See You*. Returning to England, she became a teacher at Stage Coach, teaching four- to six-year-olds and gained a degree in musical theatre at Guildford School of Acting.

Robin Millar

The man behind the singer Sade, Robin is one of the world's most successful record producers – 150 gold and platinum discs and 44 No 1 hits. Blind since childhood, he has nevertheless had an extraordinary life as a punk guitarist, photographic model, record company executive and businessman. From founding Ferrari rental companies to advising bosses of some of the world's biggest firms, to appointment as a professor at Thames Valley University, Robin is always thinking and always acting without fear. 'Adventure should be real, not imagined,' he says.

Chris Mullinder

Born in Newcastle-upon-Tyne, Chris was educated at St Joseph's Secondary Modern School and left with five O-levels.

His first job was as an office clerk, but after eight years of working in various departments he moved into sales. In 2005, he changed career again, this time into a more care-oriented profession and is now employed by an NHS trust doing clinical support work, which he finds both exciting and challenging.

He lives with his wife Cath and twin stepdaughters Rachel and Sarah in the village of Wylam, Northumberland.

James Nathan

Since winning MasterChef 2008, James Nathan has focused on turning himself into a professional chef. He began his career with Richard Corrigan at Bentley's Oyster Bar in London and then joined Michael Caines at the Bath Priory Hotel.

From an early age, James wanted to be a chef. He attended Millfield School and went on to study philosophy at King's College University, law at Manchester and took his bar finals at Lincoln's Inn, London. He practised in the criminal courts of Bristol for a year before giving up and eventually applying for MasterChef 2008.

Dave Pack

A graduate of the University of York and Guildhall School of Music in London, David is an experienced drummer and percussionist, having performed on numerous touring productions, London shows, recordings, cruise ships and panto! He has a wide musical taste and enjoys playing in a variety of settings from his work with show orchestras and classical ensembles through to his love of jazz, big band and funk. A keen pianist, David also arranges music, produces backing/click tracks and scores for use in theatre.

Contact: **davempack@yahoo.co.uk**.

Andrew Pearson

Andrew is an executive coach, trainer and facilitator to a range of industries both in the UK and overseas. He worked for twenty years in a blue chip environment before setting up as an independent consultant. He works extensively with GCC to help organisations develop effective cultures and also delivers a range of management and skill-based development programmes. His interests included painting, writing poetry and rock climbing. He is married with three grown-up children.

Laura Pelling

Laura is marketing director for a company that provides support for small businesses. She has twenty years' experience of marketing to small businesses, including developing products, leading multi-million pound brand and communication campaigns, and setting up and running small business units. Laura is married and a working mother of two teenage boys and a younger daughter. She juggles work and family commitments imperfectly to achieve the best balance she can!

Dick Pyle

Dick Pyle left Oxford University with a 'disgraceful' degree, qualified as a chartered accountant with Price Waterhouse and then launched himself into serial entrepreneurship. Adventure travel, electronic kits, management consultancy, equipment leasing, plant nursery, restaurant, natural resources, wine retailing, stockmarket research – he tried everything and 'got the T-shirt'. More failures than successes, but he did sell his leasing company to Morgan Grenfell; set up Gannock Growers, which won an RHS silver-gilt medal and exhibited at Chelsea; and Hilaire Restaurant was regularly feted by the critics; and now Truffle Tree – **www.truffle-tree.com** – and a wonderful life in South West France.

Lucy Shuker

Lucy Shuker was twenty-one when she was involved in a motorbike accident that left her paralysed from the chest down. After ten months in hospital she was discharged and ready to tackle the new challenges life threw at her. Lucy took up tennis in 2003 and never looked back. It's given her a completely different direction in her life. Lucy is currently the British number one in wheelchair tennis and travels round the world competing in tournaments, ranging from Australia through to the Far East and America, meeting new people, all with their own stories and experiences.

Anna Smółka

Anna is a highly experienced communications specialist in public and government relations. She runs a PR and consulting company, ASK PR, based in Warsaw. In addition, Anna has served as:

- corporate communications director in the Winterthur / AXA Group, Poland;
- spokeswoman and member of the Strategy Committee for Henryka Bochniarz, Polish presidential candidate in 2005;
- PR director for the largest EU pre-accession governmental campaign aimed at small and medium-sized companies;
- general director of the Polish Chamber of Press Publishers.

She is also a journalist and historian in the biggest Polish daily, *Gazeta Wyborcza*, and the opinion-leading Polish magazine *Polityka*.

Matthew Taylor

Matthew Taylor became chief executive of the Royal Society of Arts in 2006, having been chief adviser on political strategy to the prime minister.

Matthew has been a county councillor, a parliamentary candidate, a university research fellow and the director of a unit monitoring NHS policy. Until 1998, Matthew was assistant general secretary for the Labour Party. During the 1997 general election he was Labour's director of policy and a member of the party's central election strategy team. He was director of the Institute for Public Policy Research between 1999 and 2003.

Matthew is a frequent media commentator on policy and political issues.

Diana Tibble

While working as a midwife, Diana Tibble trained in counselling and homeopathy. She found that counselling within hypnosis accelerated the learning process and ability to change, so she trained in applied hypnosis and developed courses for childbirth and stress management.

She now runs a homeopathic and hypnotherapy practice in St Albans and receives referrals from midwives and GPs. She treats difficulties such as IBS, migraine, PTSD, anxiety and phobias.

Diana has given presentations to the British Society for Clinical & Academic Hypnosis and to the Royal College of Obstetrics & Gynaecology on hypnosis for childbirth.

Website: **www.innerv.net.**

Andrea (Andy) Wraith

Dentist, doctor, anaesthetist, fencer, rower, mountain marathon runner, motorbike lover, writer, pianist, animal lover, organic exponent, vegetarian, pragmatic, optimistic, feminist, believer in human and animal rights with a passion for nature, for life and freedom.

Andrea was born on a council estate in a mining village in Yorkshire. She studied medicine at Cambridge University, lectured internationally, fenced for Britain and featured on BBC 2's *Tribal Wives* series.

Her company, ASA MedCare, is based in Harley Street, London.

Her passion? Exploring new ideas and skills to feed that deep urge to spread her wings and become all she is capable of!

Contact: **andrea.wraith@asamedcare.co.uk.**
Website: **www.asamedcare.co.uk.**

Acknowledgements

This is a special book for me. It brings together all the different phases of my life. As a serial achiever, I have been through the process you will read about many times and each step has given me something new. Sometimes, the benefits were obvious, occasionally it took a while for the penny to drop. Writing this book has shown me just how much I've gained from success *and* failure.

In terms of writing the book, there have been two outstanding people. First, my husband John who came up with the original thought – 'Why do some people go from peak to peak in their lives, while others give up after one?' Without John as a support, backup and sounding board, I'm not sure the book would ever have been written. Second, Stephen Partridge has been my first reader – identifying when ideas worked and letting me know when it just didn't make sense – but always leaving me laughing.

The serial achievers themselves have been an enormous help. By telling their stories, they helped refine my thinking, so I could develop the fundamentals and behaviours you find here. They have been generous and extremely impressive in their own right. You can read a short biography about each one in the About the contributors section and I'm sure their stories will fascinate you.

Very important – my daughter and grandson visited at regular intervals to keep my feet on the ground. Matthew Fowler acted as a guinea pig and tried out exercises for me, sharing his ongoing journey to success. And my youngest daughter just always believed in me – which has been worth its weight in gold.

Sue Simmons, my personal asistant, has been a great support throughout, organising my time and helping me manage the process.

Finally, Sam Jackson, my editor at Prentice Hall, who shared my excitement for the concept of serial achievement and success. She, too, believed in me and supported me in delivering a book that I hope will add real value and help you make the very best of your core talent.

Introduction

Are you ready for success?

Some people just seem to be naturally successful. They use their skills and talent in different ways, discovering more about themselves and reaching one peak after another. The effect is cumulative – as they achieve, they learn; and as they learn, they develop their ability so can achieve more, which means they learn more, and so it goes on. As a result, they end up accomplishing infinitely more than they ever thought possible. It is an exciting, challenging and very successful approach to life. I call them serial achievers.

In fact, they are not superhuman. They are just people like you and me who have learned how to free themselves from the restraints that hold others back. They have learned that the worst regret is for the things you didn't do, the chances you didn't take. So they have gone with the opportunities that presented themselves – through both tough and exciting times – and made the most of them. As a result, they will never suffer the nagging dissatisfaction that things could have – should have – been better.

Are you willing to be that successful? Making the most of the talent and skills you have? Going from one peak to another in your life?

If you really want to, you can certainly do it.

It will require you to push the boundary of what you presently know to be true. It may result in using your life quite differently, doing work that you had never thought of before or developing your present work way beyond your dreams. As long as you are up for that challenge, then go for it! After all, in our fast moving and dynamic world, staying still is not really an option. The ongoing discovery and development that serial achievers live by is the perfect way to stay ahead of the field.

"In our fast moving world, staying still is not an option."

There is always more to you, so make the most of it

At eighty years old, my father believed he'd wasted his life. By most standards he was a successful man. He had a good career, was full of verve and energy and he left a strong legacy in the world. The problem was his belief that he could have done more.

For him, the highlight was his years in the Fleet Air Arm during the war – to his mind, this was when he really flowered. It became 'the time of his life' and he held on to it until the end. The constant comparison stopped him taking satisfaction from later achievements – he could only see what might have been. He felt the emptiness of unrealised potential and it haunted him.

Of course, although he only admitted it in his old age, the problem had always been there. Like many of his generation he chose to manage his dissatisfaction and accept his life path, without actively seeking to change. But clues appeared continually over the years, in subtle feelings of frustration, in longings for something different.

The clues are there for you too – in those moments of clarity, emotion and excitement that make clear you are bigger than you ever thought possible. Ignore them at your peril, because therein lie your own seeds of regret. Of course, this doesn't mean the hints and nudges will always work out as you hope.

Sometimes you may try and fail – but at least you tried and you will certainly have learned. And that knowledge will prepare you for your next challenge, your next life chapter.

The X-factor

Are we talking here about the elusive 'X-factor' that so fascinates us all? Indeed we are, but that doesn't mean you have to sacrifice yourself on the altar of Saturday night television or on the front pages of a tabloid newspaper. The popular idea of success has become rooted in fame and money, but there is so much more to it than that.

We are looking for your own personal X-factor. The core talent that can take you on a lifelong journey of success and discovery. You definitely have talent – it's up to you whether you use it or not. And that is what this book is all about – working your core talent so you fulfil your promise and become as successful as you want to be.

Serial achievers

The important thing to remember is that your core talent can deliver more than one thing, which is useful since nothing in life is constant. Neither is what we want out of it. This is part of the excitement. The world we live in now is too fast and furious for just one life vision.

This is where the concept of serial achievement comes in. Don't think about your present vision of success as 'it' for life. It is right for now *and* you will almost certainly change completely in the years to come. I was fifty before I wrote my first book, while at thirty it wasn't even on my radar. Core talent will offer all sorts of outlets in a lifetime, once you understand what that talent really is.

Start thinking this way and life immediately opens up. You no longer have to know 'what you want to do when you grow up'. You just have to know what you want to do *now*. That's good enough – you can leave the rest until later, by which time you'll be ready for whatever the next step needs to be.

The test of a life well used

In preparing to write this book, I spoke to a lot of people who have achieved great things in their lives. You won't know most of them because this is not about fame, it's about doing what matters to them and doing it well.

A common feature was the moment of realisation that they had to take responsibility for their own lives. They couldn't expect anyone else to do it for them. It was generally a tough time that flicked the switch – interestingly, failing at school was a common one – and they saw in glorious Technicolor that if they didn't get on and sort themselves out, then nothing was going to happen. So they did – and it did. Some successes, some failures, plenty of learning and always the sense of a lot more to come.

Just in case you haven't had one of those moments yet or at least never focused on it, try the test of a life well used. The question it poses is this:

> *When you review your life from the vantage point of old age, will you be satisfied?*

> *Will you be without regret, knowing that you made the very best use of your time?*

Sit quietly for a moment and imagine you are ninety years old, looking back over your life, checking to see if you used it well. See it as a film – the highs, the lows, the challenges and successes. And as you see each picture pass before you, notice how you feel:

Do you feel elated/excited/satisfied?

Or

Do you think 'if only'/ I should have/why on earth didn't I!

Now focus on this present chapter of your life – as you look back at today from your armchair with ninety years of wisdom, how does it look? What gives you a sense of satisfaction? And what causes you to feel regret because you never acted/spoke out/took a risk?

"There is still time to do something about it."

If you could put your lifetime of successes and regrets on a pair of scales, which way would they fall? If it's towards the negative, then thank heaven you took a look now – there is still time to do something about it. And if you are gloriously overweighed with success, don't sit back, there is still more out there – even if you actually are ninety!

How to use this book

This book is born out of my own experience and that of the many people I met in my life, plus the exciting serial achievers who told me their stories so I could share them with you. It is a book about hope and life. I really believe that we can all be successful, as long as we are pointing in the right direction, are open to the opportunities around us and prepared to do what it takes to seize them. There is nothing weird or wonderful about this – that's what makes it so exciting. It's something we all know how to do if we just let ourselves pay attention to what matters most.

If you are working in an organisation and managing serial achievers, this book will help you understand how they function. Look on **www.thepsychologyofsuccess.co.uk** for an article that translates the psychology of success into the working environment, ensuring that you can make the most of the talented people that work for you.

Whatever your purpose, you can learn from the 'tricks of the trade' according to serial achievers.

The five fundamentals

Exploring the five fundamentals will provide you with essential learning about yourself:

- **First Fundamental: Know your style** – understand your own achiever style and learn how to use this to your best advantage.

- **Second Fundamental: Get a grip of your personal gravity** – understand the life patterns that help you move forward as a serial achiever and learn how to address those that hold you back.

- **Third Fundamental: Harness your life alignment curve** – work through the process that underpins each life chapter, discovering where you are now and how to move to the next stage.

- **Fourth Fundamental: Discover your core talent** – identify your core talent, that essential element of serial achievement that provides opportunities for you to perform and deliver in a wide range of scenarios.

- **Fifth Fundamental: Address your needs** – explore the basic needs of the serial achiever and learn how to put these in place for yourself.

Working your way through the fundamentals will give you the grounding you need to move forward as a serial achiever. Once you have this knowledge, the behaviours give you the presence you need in the world.

The seven behaviours

The seven behaviours will take you into any situation
core talent demands. Using them on a regular basis
you deliver this life chapter and get ready for the next:

- **Behaviour One: Take responsibility** – only you can take the steps
  to being a serial achiever. The moment you take this on board,
  then you are on your way.

- **Behaviour Two: Build relationships** – people are the key to
  success, so understand the drivers of great interactions and use
  them to build mutually beneficial connections.

- **Behaviour Three: Embrace change** – don't just wait for change
  to occur, go out and find it! Use this fast changing society to
  your advantage.

- **Behaviour Four: Invite opportunity** – understand how to put
  yourself in the way of opportunity and spot what is right in
  front of you.

- **Behaviour Five: Be passionate** – use your excitement and
  enthusiasm to help you move directly towards your next life
  chapter.

- **Behaviour Six: Be conscious** – identify your next challenge or
  project, then clarify the skills you need and set about
  developing them.

- **Behaviour Seven: Get focused** – choose where to place your
  energy, so you reach your goals and prepare for the next life
  chapter.

Start now!

You may want to read from start to finish or you may be a 'dipper'.
Both are fine, except do work out your core talent early on
(Fourth Fundamental), since this is the key to your achievement.

stories and exercises will set you thinking and you'll have loads of ideas as you go along. Many of them will be really important and you'll be quite sure you won't forget them. But believe me, as the next light bulb comes on, the previous idea will be pushed so far back you may lose it for a while. So get yourself a notebook and let it be your confidante. Keep it somewhere safe and use it as you wish – draw, write, mind map – whatever works for you.

Tracking the process will be part of the adventure. Not only will you hold on to good ideas, the patterns of your life will become clear, making it much easier to take the next steps productively.

So let's begin – there are only positives out there for you to find!

Part 1

Five fundamentals

FIRST FUNDAMENTAL

Know your style

BE CLEAR WHAT YOU WANT AND HOW YOU TICK

'In the past I have focused too much on what I'm good at. When I also focus on what I'm *not* good at, then I am most successful.' For Robin Millar, an eminent record producer, this key piece of honesty has stood him in good stead.

Understanding what drives you is essential if you want to be successful. Just as you won't get far by putting petrol in a diesel-powered car, so you'll struggle to attain personal goals if you don't understand what fuels your drive and determination. Couple that understanding with learning from serial achievers and you will make the most of your gifts by clarifying the opportunities that will work best.

There are three elements that influence your style:

- what success looks like for you;
- your relationship to risk and dissatisfaction;
- what sort of achiever you are.

Understanding success

The first step is to define what success looks like for you.

For Lucy Shuker, it is pushing beyond her limitations – going on to the next level, whether that is taking the No 1 slot in tennis or mastering the movement from wheelchair to sofa easily on her own.

For Naaz Coker, it is about being the best and knowing she is the best. Her way of responding to a new challenge is to gather all the learning she can through academia, which provides affirmation at the same time.

And for Mark Barnard, success is bringing up a happy family, being healthy and building a good business. Oh, and trying something new each week, so keeping his learning going and always moving forward.

"Serial achievers want to test themselves and deliver the very best."

Serial achievers all have their own definitions of success, with the common feature that they want to test themselves and deliver the very best – that's where their personal fulfilment comes from. Whatever your role, there is a real buzz in being appreciated or seeing your efforts make a positive impact on others.

What do we mean by success?

First of all, what we are talking about here is *your* idea of success, not what other people believe or expect of you. Their definition will always be based on their own measure, which may be very different to yours, so let's put them on one side for now.

The symbols of success vary from one person to another and from one time to another. Getting the degree you want or running the marathon in the allotted time are goals that give you something to reach for. They are also tangible measures that others can see and respect, which is always gratifying.

The intangibles of success are more subtle. They span your life to this point and include your hopes and fears for the future. When it comes down to having a successful life or not, then the essence remains the same for all of us.

The success equation

Security + Challenge + Fulfilment = Success

The three factors of the success equation are consistent, but the weighting will vary according to the individual and what drives them. For some, security is a major factor in whether they feel positive about their lives; for others having a consistent challenge is high on the list. Weighting will also change over time. For example, turning sixty may bring a totally different horizon – with the mortgage paid, the pension taken care of and the kids running their own lives, the way is clear for some very exciting challenges.

Security

We are most aware of the importance of security when we don't have it. If you have ever experienced a time when your livelihood or home was at risk, then you know what I mean. Those moments bring into sharp focus the importance of your own front door and the money for food.

A home to call your own, enough money to live the life you want, relationships that nurture and sustain you, plus health and wellbeing – these are the things that give you the freedom to achieve in your life.

Getting your priorities right

Lucy is a beautiful young woman who has always loved her sport. From her early years she was at her happiest out on the playing fields and especially around horses.

Her other great love was biking, so with her first pay packet she arranged tuition, took her test and bought a motor bike. She had twelve days of bliss, exploring the countryside in a new way. Then the curtain came down and she found herself in hospital with a broken back.

Being a naturally cheery person, against all the odds, she still managed to keep up her positive attitude for much of the time. It was worst, alone at night, with no one to distract her. Then she came face to face with her fears about being a paraplegic. Hard as it is for others to understand, she has come through it and is incredibly strong – even to the point of acknowledging how good her life is right now.

Day-to-day security has a totally different meaning for Lucy – managing herself has to come first, including the three hours it takes to get up in the morning. Yet she hasn't let that stop her. Through good planning and determination, she takes on each challenge as it arises, including reaching a top ten world ranking in wheelchair tennis.

So watch this space – she could well be that grand slam champion the UK keeps hoping for!

To free yourself up to be successful, identify the essentials that make *you* feel secure and allow you to take the actions you want to, eg:

- having a committed group of friends;
- eating a healthy diet;
- behaving appropriately at work;
- paying the bills on time.

While some of these may feel like a chore, they could be just the thing to free you up for an exciting challenge.

If security carries a high weighting in the equation for you, then the chores may just be the beginning. A feeling of sanctuary and comfort enables some people to take on the other elements of success more effectively. Laura Pelling is a great believer in building the environment she needs to take on change. Even sitting in a coffee shop to do a bit of work, she will create her own space by putting out her Blackberry, phone and notebook.

I'm sure you will have your own particular requirement. Achieving success means paying attention to what you need and taking that seriously.

Challenge

It is challenge that helps us grow and develop. While not always pleasant, without it life becomes repetitive and a bit dull – even the most amazing tasks become ordinary when done day after day. Challenge also enables us to measure how we are doing and to find out more about who we are, providing a good reminder of strengths.

"It is challenge that helps us grow and develop."

We all find different ways to challenge ourselves – to explore just how far we can go:

- Some people take on additional learning – like Naaz who took on an MBA.
- Some take up a new pastime – Argentinean tango is the new salsa.
- Others go for a career change – like Chris Mullinder who went from being a successful salesman to training as a nursery nurse.

It doesn't need to be big time – playing in the local five-a-side football team is a gratifying challenge on Sunday afternoon when the rest of the week is static and desk bound. Just don't expect it all to be exciting and fun. Learning an instrument or joining Weight Watchers will be boring, demanding and satisfying in turn, requiring you to stick at it even when you just want to go home and watch television. But the day you join a band or go into a trendy shop to buy an outfit will feel immensely rewarding!

And then there are the challenges that life brings, whether you like them or not. The company cutting back that has decided your department has to go, the partner that prefers another person, or illness that strikes you out of the blue. These sound as if they have little to do with success, but in fact they are central.

A consistent theme for serial achievers is that challenge is a great learning tool – the lesson that life has to give you. You can either welcome it or bury your head in the sand – either way it will affect your day-to-day existence. Only when you look back will you see the real value and it is then that you can review how you did:

- Did you take the learning and grow?
- Or did you sit back and hope it would go away?

Your sense of success and achievement will be determined by which one you choose.

Fulfilment

Keeping the home fires burning, as well as taking on challenges, is demanding. But when you believe you have made a good job of it, the sense of fulfilment is enormous.

The ability to make that honest assessment of effectiveness is a major contributor to success. It helps you to:

- clarify where you were successful;
- identify your next area of learning and challenge;
- validate your ability.

Setting goals helps focus your mind on where you are going, not to mention the fact that arriving at the destination allows you to stop and celebrate. It doesn't need to be a big event – whatever feels like celebration to you – but make sure you do it. You are the one who knows just how much effort you have put in, so enjoy the fruits of your labour.

For some people this is really hard to do. They are so concerned that they are not up to standard that they give all their attention to the next challenge, never stopping to notice how well they have done. The end result is that life becomes one long struggle with no let-up and stress can easily take over.

So think back to your last success – how well did you celebrate? Did you delight in the outputs – admiring your achievement, sharing it with others and taking time out to relax? Or did you just cross it off the list and move on?

EXPLORATION

Review yourself against the success equation using the table below as a guide and find out what matters to you. Remember, there is no right or wrong in this. The task is to understand exactly what makes you feel successful, so you can use the data to inform your decisions.

Security	Challenge	Fulfilment
Identify the aspects of life that allow you to feel secure, eg:	Consider how you respond to moments of challenge. Do you:	Think about times of fulfilment. Do you:
▓ Home	▓ Avoid them	▓ Seek them out
▓ Family	▓ Use them well	▓ Remember them fondly
▓ Secure job	▓ Find them difficult	▓ Find them difficult
▓ Independence at work	▓ Learn from them	▓ Celebrate well
▓ Good health	▓ Seek them out	▓ Include others
▓ Affectionate pet	▓ Use them as motivation	▓ Appreciate the learning
▓ Good friends		
▓ Regular holidays		
% importance	% importance	% importance

Look through each of the three boxes in the table and decide which you value most. Divide 100 marks between the three. This will give you the percentage importance you place on each area.

Some people will have a 50/25/25 split because they don't feel able to move into the unknown until they feel secure. Some will have a 10/70/20 balance because they thrive on challenge – it is the stuff of life to them. Others will work on 10/50/40 – they are good at taking on challenges, then set aside time to revel in the moment of success. You will read about all types in this book.

It doesn't matter what your balance is. The important thing is to understand so you can tend your life accordingly. This is the way to greater achievement.

When you have a clear idea of your personal equation, undertake a review of your life to date and consider how successful you have been against your own equation. If you are lacking in a specific area, think about your present occupation and consider how you might shift the balance to improve your chance of success.

Relationship to risk and dissatisfaction

While everyone can achieve, they certainly won't all do it in the same way. You will have gathered by now that different elements drive different people – heaven forbid that we should all be the same!

There are two factors that determine how we go about achieving in our lives:

■ The willingness to take calculated risk.

■ The ability to manage dissatisfaction.

The willingness to take calculated risk

Risk is a constant in life – we are surrounded by it. Yet some people manage it more effectively than others.

Dick Pyle is the perfect example of someone who enjoys risk. A serial entrepreneur, he accepts that he must make mistakes if he wants to get anywhere. 'If you do nothing you will certainly never make a mistake. Do anything and you are bound to get something wrong. Don't make them twice – that's the thing – learn from them.'

"Do anything and you are bound to get something wrong."

In contrast, Bill (*name changed*) won't go within a million miles of what he perceives as risk. Stuck in a job he hates and convinced that he is no good, he slogs on day after day waiting for the axe to fall.

Of course, in his determination not to rock the boat he causes more problems. Truly risk averse people spend their lives trying to blend into the scenery and hoping no one will notice them. This 'shrinking violet' mentality leaves others with no option but to make decisions without them – and there is a risk that the outcomes won't include those who fail to contribute.

In fact, you can't avoid risk in your life. Just by walking across the road you take a risk. We know this in theory, but rarely think about it. The same goes for many risks that face us on a day-to-day basis. The key is to see that:

- We manage risk best when we take responsibility for it.
- Blaming others increases the risk, by giving away responsibility and therefore control.

'It all depends how you classify risk,' according to Peter Fisher. 'The more you know, the less risk you are taking. You have enough information about something that other people might consider a risk, so for you it isn't.'

This is a common theme with serial achievers. How the world sees them and how they see themselves are entirely different things. Once you have the knowledge and information you need, you can step into the unknown, even when those watching think you are stepping over a precipice.

EXPLORATION

1. Draw a route map of your life to date. You can do this a number of ways:

   a. Think of it as a river course – put in the babbling brook stage, the rapids and white water times, the sections of smooth flow that supports boats and fun sports . . .

   b. A road journey is also a good metaphor – the long clear motorways, the traffic jams and accident black spots, the busy, exciting city roads and the quiet and peaceful country lanes.

   c. Or just any way of representing your life that works for you.

   Include the turning points, the tough times and happy times in your life.

2. Put a circle around those times when you realised you were taking a risk and make a few notes about how you managed it.

3. Look back with the magic of hindsight and identify those times/situations that were in fact a risk, even though you didn't realise it. What was the result?

4. Think about what stopped you seeing those risks at the time, eg:

   a. Fear of the implications.

   b. Fixation on a specific outcome.

   c. Determination to be right.

5. What does this process say about your relationship to risk? Do you:

    a. Thrive on risk?

    b. Accept and manage it?

    c. Avoid it at all costs and then regret?

The ability to manage dissatisfaction

Life is a real rollercoaster ride. The good times are fabulous – and they come and go, along with the tough experiences. Hard though this is to accept, there is little we can do about it – we all have to manage dissatisfaction at regular intervals.

If we hold a view that the rollercoaster is life putting opportunities in front of us, then we look for the best way to manage situations as they arise. Some people do this very well and others appear to struggle.

"The rollercoaster is life putting opportunities in front of us."

The way of managing dissatisfaction varies according to personal style:

- Investigative: some people hit a tough spot and go all out to find options that will get them out of it.
- Introspective: others look inwards to understand what happened in an attempt to define the next step.

Both are valid ways of working and both will reach a final outcome, they are just different processes.

Investigative
Investigative people take on dissatisfaction as a challenge. They look at the cause of the problem and then cast around for ideas

that will help them. They may feel downcast at having to manage the change, but this won't last long – they will soon be on the track of action that will enable them to see a more comfortable future.

To achieve this, they:

■ Analyse the situation to understand exactly what happened to cause the problem. Then retrieve the positives and address the negatives.

■ Approach the same situation from a different perspective. Businesses that stop and look at the problem from the customer's perspective are doing just this – it gives them a different view and opens up their thinking.

■ Leave the situation and go somewhere else. This may be a new job, new relationship or new home. All actions that redefine the moment and take away the unpleasant feelings.

Once Andy Wraith started working as a newly qualified dentist she soon realised it wasn't for her. 'I had so much more to give – it felt like a waste.' She couldn't see how to move forward, so looked for something totally different that she might like to do. 'I came up with scuba diving, archery and fencing. I tried fencing first, found I had a talent for it and really enjoyed it.' It helped her manage six months of dissatisfaction, keeping her upbeat, fresh and open to new opportunities. By which time she discovered her fascination with dental anaesthesia and found a whole new direction.

Introspective

Introspective serial achievers turn to their own feelings and reactions as a way of understanding the world and coping with dissatisfaction. In the early stages, this can leave them feeling concerned, worried and anxious about the situation and how they have contributed. 'Personal gravity' (Second Fundamental) comes fully into play, so they can't always see the wood for the trees.

This is a tough time, yet they manage to contain their dissatisfaction and carry on with life as usual. This may not be a conscious choice, just an inability to see the right way out that leaves every possibility feeling like an enormous risk.

They deal with this in different ways:

- Setting aside time for reflection and review of the situation, working out exactly what happened to create the discomfort. This works well for more introverted people who need time to think. It will help them gain the understanding they need to make informed choices.

- Finding a good friend or colleague to explore the problem with. This is useful for those who learn through talking. It also works well when the situation is entrenched – finding solutions from the mindset that created the problem is not always an easy one. However, supporters must beware – introspective people will not come to a quick decision, so it could be a frustrating experience!

- Carrying on as if nothing has happened and letting nature takes its course. The dissatisfaction will finally grow to a pitch that brings an answer with it and change happens anyway.

"Finding solutions from the mindset that created the problem is not always easy."

Laura Pelling is big on taking responsibility for every problem that comes her way. Her first reaction is that she should have done more and must do more now. It makes her a really safe pair of hands and the very best person to deliver to a deadline. The downside is that she can easily overdo it.

She hates failing, so assuming she has to be the one to act gives her back some control. Talking things through with her executive coach increased her understanding. 'At least I know now that if I don't stop, I will internally combust. And I have also learned to harness that drive to help me succeed, but without ruining my health!'

Varying style

Despite your personal preference, some situations call for a different reaction, eg:

- An emotional upheaval such as a death, divorce or redundancy will cause a time of introspection, whatever your preference.

- An expected change that is exciting and timely will call for a review of the options, without time for introspection.

Investigative to Introspective. Investigators will move quickly to an answer to stop that feeling of discomfort. Mostly this will work, but sometimes it is an avoidance mechanism. Persistent avoidance means the problem just hangs around waiting to be sorted out. Eventually, the investigator has to stop and look inwards for the answer.

Introspective to Investigative. When a situation requires fast action and a choice between specific options, the introspective type can come unstuck. Their ability to manage dissatisfaction will tempt them into waiting to see what happens. In fact, they need to consciously raise a sense of urgency and refocus to see the options. Once they do this, they are able to reach a decision.

EXPLORATION

1. Return to the route map of your life and identify the times of dissatisfaction. They may correlate to your times of risk or they may be different.

2. Choose the most significant one and give some thought to the way you handled it. Did you:

a. Investigate: think through the benefits and risks, making lists about the different ways you could handle it?

b. Introspect: feel miserable or depressed, reviewing how you contributed to the problem, before coming up with how you felt the situation should be handled?

3. From the timeline: with hindsight, where do you see the problem beginning? How long was it before you realised what was happening?

4. From the timeline: how long were you *actually* feeling dissatisfied? And how does that compare with how long you *felt* you were in a rough patch?

From this exercise, decide whether you use investigation or introspection to identify the next step.

What sort of achiever are you?

Put these two factors of calculated risk and managing dissatisfaction together and it is possible to define three types of achiever:

- stable achiever;
- consistent achiever;
- serial achiever.

Given the findings from your exploration into calculated risk and dissatisfaction, look at the different styles in Figure 1.1 and see where you are in your life just now.

Stable achiever

Steady and active stable achievers are extremely important people in our fast moving world. They keep us all going, acting reliably to deliver what is needed. They like to feel comfortable, so are very good at setting boundaries and defining what they will and won't put up with. When in doubt, they get busy with

Figure 1.1   Achiever styles

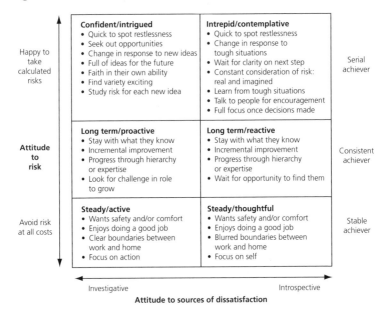

Attitude to risk		
Happy to take calculated risks	**Confident/intrigued** • Quick to spot restlessness • Seek out opportunities • Change in response to new ideas • Full of ideas for the future • Faith in their own ability • Find variety exciting • Study risk for each new idea	**Intrepid/contemplative** • Quick to spot restlessness • Change in response to tough situations • Wait for clarity on next step • Constant consideration of risk: real and imagined • Learn from tough situations • Talk to people for encouragement • Full focus once decisions made	Serial achiever
Attitude to risk	**Long term/proactive** • Stay with what they know • Incremental improvement • Progress through hierarchy or expertise • Look for challenge in role to grow	**Long term/reactive** • Stay with what they know • Incremental improvement • Progress through hierarchy or expertise • Wait for opportunity to find them	Consistent achiever
Avoid risk at all costs	**Steady/active** • Wants safety and/or comfort • Enjoys doing a good job • Clear boundaries between work and home • Focus on action	**Steady/thoughtful** • Wants safety and/or comfort • Enjoys doing a good job • Blurred boundaries between work and home • Focus on self	Stable achiever
	Investigative	Introspective	

Attitude to sources of dissatisfaction

activities that return them to an even keel. They have their own ways of working and a clear personal style that they are happy with.

The value of stable achievers

Sally (*name changed*) is a perfect example of a steady/active stable achiever. Working as PA to a serial achiever, she is in her element. She acts as the glue and foundation that allows her boss to go out and about in the world, trying different things and discovering new opportunities.

Sally doesn't like feeling uncomfortable, it's the last thing she wants. She manages this by setting a very clear boundary around what she will do. This way, she knows what to expect in life and can make the plans she needs. She handles uncertainty by dealing with what she can and putting the rest on one side until she has more information – there is little point in thinking about something she can't change!

If the demands of work take her outside of that boundary, then the risk level increases and Sally will become stressed. However, hard work is not a problem, so she focuses on clearing the decks in order to get life back on an even keel.

As long as her boss doesn't push the boundary too much, then there is real satisfaction for Sally in doing a good job and seeing success emerge.

Steady and thoughtful stable achievers are also important people who keep the day-to-day work going. They gain pleasure from doing a good job, putting in a vast amount of energy to ensure quality. At times, this means they will blur the boundaries between work and home life, burning the midnight oil to ensure they can deliver. When the going gets tough, they focus on themselves and how they are affected, which can lead to stress and anxiety. Eventually, they will clarify their boundaries, deciding exactly how much they are willing to change. At this point they will regain equilibrium.

Consistent achievers

Consistent achievers are high performers. Really good at their jobs, they have the capacity to focus on the work that needs to be done. While not keen to move far outside their comfort zone, they do want to keep improving so take risks within that zone. This means they will progress well within their field. They enjoy the challenge, alongside the familiarity of a specific way of working.

Long term/reactive consistent achievers are very conscious of their customers and build strong relationships from the outset. On the look out for ways of improving the quality of their work, they deliver exceptional service and people want them to continue. They manage dissatisfaction well, so when they are fed up and ready to move on, no one will ever know!

The risk in containing dissatisfaction

Josh (*name changed*) is a brilliant long term/reactive consistent achiever. He has carved a niche for himself as a consultant in construction. Well regarded, he is never short of an assignment and he delivers exceptional quality to his clients.

Because he waits for opportunities to come to him, he is never confident about his business. He can be working hard with a full diary, fearing that by next month there will be nothing there for him to do. In fact, work always does come in and he rarely has time to himself, but he doesn't want to take that for granted.

The real problem for Josh is that he contains dissatisfaction for longer than is good for him. For years he has been saying that he is fed up with the work, but the level of his expertise provides a good life, so it is hard to branch out into pastures new. He will take a risk, within reason. The end result is that his friends know he is unhappy, while his clients think he is the best thing since sliced bread. And nothing is ever likely to change.

Long term/proactive consistent achievers have a similar approach to Josh in that they will be brilliant at delivering quality outputs in their work. The difference is that they don't want life to be uncomfortable, so will take action pretty quickly to stay on an even keel. They have found a style that works, so they set out to repeat it when the going gets tough – in a different place, at a different level or for a different boss.

Consistent achievers will:

- stay in the same organisation, moving up through the ranks and away from a boss, employee or colleague they find difficult;
- find another way of working that uses the same skills, but reduces the risk factor;
- take on the risk and work to settle it down as soon as possible.

Again, these are great people to have around because they know what they are doing. They will always deliver and will, on the whole, be good to work with.

Serial achievers

Serial achievers just love to learn about themselves and life. They want to keep moving forward and stretching themselves into the next challenge. Willing to take calculated risk, they don't hold on to the familiar for its own sake. Their drive is to be the best and make sure they access all their talent and gifts.

Confident/intrigued serial achievers know quickly when they have reached the end of the road with a job or a project. They thoroughly dislike dissatisfaction and are brilliant at coming up with new ideas for how to get round it or away from it. Ideas flow out of them and they are keen to get going. They enjoy the challenge and variety – even when the ideas don't work, they are persistent and just pick themselves up and try again.

Seeing life as an opportunity

Tunde Banjoko is a perfect example of a confident/intrigued serial achiever who sets out to find alternative opportunities. Growing up on a tough estate in London, he had a wonderful mother who gave him strong values and plenty of support. In contrast, the absence of his father at an early age meant his prime role models were men on the streets, who showed him how to survive, but also helped identify that this was not what he wanted for himself.

Life was never easy. Living as a black man in the UK, he learned early that he had to stick up for himself. His good brain enabled him to get what he called a 'boozers' degree – plenty of partying, a bit of study the night before the exam and a mark that scraped through. The arrival of his first child ignited his determination to provide a strong role model, so he set out to find a good job that would bring him prospects.

- He began working in insurance, servicing policies. He did well and liked the idea of accounts, but the manager didn't support him, so he looked for another job.

- He really wanted to be a trader, so sent out over 200 letters to banks. It was taking out the word 'black' that meant he finally got a couple of interviews. One manager agreed to take him on, despite the fact that he would be the only person of colour, but the job was soulless.

- Next up was a job in advertising, which took him through to a sales job. After two tough years, he was made redundant.

- Another sales job and another redundancy, driving a mini cab and taking an HNC qualification in information technology, brought him to a job advert asking for someone to set up an employment initiative to help others get into work. He took the job on for a few months – or so he told himself.

Local Employment Access Projects (LEAP) has become a highly successful organisation that helps people get into jobs. Not only does it teach participants how to get a job, it empowers them so they are ready to work when they get there.

Tunde's willingness to go after opportunities and make changes in himself and his attitude meant that he found his way to something meaningful. He was also driven by his idea of what the future needed to look like – not least for his own family – and this vision for the future will keep him striving.

Intrepid/contemplative serial achievers respond very differently to the challenges that life has to bring. Their capacity to manage dissatisfaction means they mine a rich seam of personal learning each time a challenge arrives on the scene. Their response is an emotional one in the first instance, causing them to turn inwards to understand what it going on.

It can be an agonising wait for those watching, because only when the situation becomes unbearable will the achiever take action.

If this is how you work, expect other people to struggle when you do finally make your move. To their mind you were in the pit of despair yesterday and suddenly today you are on a mission! They will have to catch up and because they haven't had the benefit of all your brewing time, they may question your judgement. Don't be upset and don't doubt yourself, just give them the information they need and suggest they enjoy the ride.

Can you change your style?

The thorny question is: can you move to serial achiever or do you have to stay in the same box forever?

The answer is: it all depends on what you really want:

- If a particular style is your nature, then you may prefer to stay where you are. However, life will challenge you at some point – in which case you have an opportunity to change – if you want it enough.

- If you have got into a habit of behaving in a particular way, you may be settled, but uncomfortable. You can use your discomfort as a trigger to change.

- You may know right now that you are not happy and want to be a serial achiever – in which case you can definitely change.

"It all depends on what you really want."

Please note: you can shift up and down from one box to another if you are willing to put in the effort. However, it is unusual to cross from one side of the matrix to the other, because the tendency to be either investigative or introspective is deeply embedded. So if you are a long term/reactive person, you can move to intrepid/contemplative. You would have difficulty in moving to confident/intrigued because that would require you to change your style fundamentally.

Moving from one place to another demands that you first learn more about yourself. Once you understand your personal gravity (Second Fundamental) and core talent (Fourth Fundamental) you will be ready to employ the serial achiever attributes to good effect.

Success and serial achievement

The secret of a life well used is to develop your talent, using every ounce of potential, because only then will you feel satisfied that you have done your best.

Fulfilling potential needs a willingness to step periodically into the unknown, as you develop yourself and your ability. To the outside world that looks risky. To serial achievers the risk is well calculated – they have worked out what to expect and decided they are up for the challenge.

This book is all about the psychology that lies behind that process of using risk well, so you are successful in what you do. It is about setting up the environment that will support you, then using the behaviours that will lead you to multiple peaks and a successful life.

Where are you now?

Having been introduced to the concept of serial achievement, you will have a clear idea of your own personal style. You will understand:

- the success factors you need to achieve in your life;
- your own relationship to risk;
- your ability to manage dissatisfaction;
- the different styles of achievement, decided which box you are

in and whether that is your place of safety or just a short resting place.

As you ponder on all these factors, keep writing notes about your findings. Remember that words of wisdom are often the first ones to get lost, so capture them while you can.

SECOND FUNDAMENTAL

Get a grip of your personal gravity

KNOW THE POWER OF YOUR PERSONAL HISTORY AND MAKE IT WORK FOR YOU

Peter Fisher still remembers his old school motto: 'They used to have it on the stage. "Aim high and be satisfied with nothing but the best." I found that interesting and it is burnt into my head!' Looking at Peter's career as a social worker, business leader and investor, it is clear the concept stood him in good stead.

We all have mottos and mindsets that were 'burnt into our heads' from an early age – some are useful like Peter's and others hold us back from making the most of our potential. We also develop new beliefs as we go through life, based on our positive and negative experiences. Altogether, they determine what we believe is possible and how we think about our own ability. This is our personal gravity.

Personal gravity

We all know gravity. We don't all understand how it works, or frankly, even care. We just take for granted that there is enough of it to stop us floating off into space and not so much that we can't move. Gravity defines what is and what is not physically possible in this world. We just accept that and get on with it – 'that's life' we say.

It is much the same in the realm of personal gravity. It defines what is possible in our personal world and since we don't really understand how it works, we just get on with it, saying 'that's life'. Until it starts to go wrong – when we start feeling weighed down or notice that we're just drifting along aimlessly. Then we begin to question why.

The difference is that, unlike physical gravity, we can control the settings of our personal gravity. We can choose whether 'that's life' or not. We are responsible for creating our own personal gravity and, as a result, for defining what is possible in the world we inhabit – the world in which we live our lives. To do that, however, we need to understand how it works.

There are three different elements that combine to form personal gravity:

- mindsets and mottos;
- familiarity;
- life pressure.

The three areas overlap and mix together to provide us with a strong foundation for 'how we live our lives'. By giving us parameters to work within, they enable us to get on with life in a more or less comfortable way (Figure 2.1).

Figure 2.1 Personal gravity

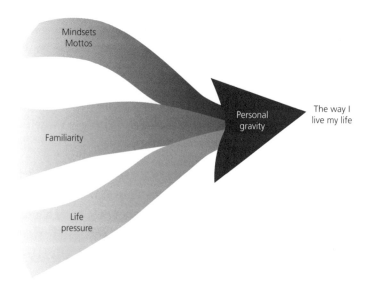

Mindsets and mottos

From our earliest days we are affected by what happens around us. We learn by paying attention to what works and doing it again. So at six weeks a baby will realise that moving its mouth in a particular way brings more cuddles and a lot more attention, so they do it again and are soon smiling like a professional.

The way we see life around us becomes the norm and we make assumptions that this is right, based on our personal experience. As soon as school enters the frame we develop another set of 'rules'. We choose what we pay attention to according to how it makes us feel:

- behaviour that leads us to feel valued and accepted will be repeated;
- actions that bring negative feelings are assumed to be wrong, so we give them up;
- behaviour that means we fit into the norm and look like everyone else go to the top of the list.

We literally 'set our minds' to behave in a particular way. It makes life easy by reducing the number of decisions to be made; although it also means that we can get into a habit and miss opportunities because they fall outside of what we expect to see.

"We literally 'set our minds' to behave in a particular way."

Mottos are the well-worn phrases we adopt from respected figures in our lives, such as parents, teachers and special friends. Most go back to our formative years and occasionally we design new ones in later life. They form our life philosophies, so shape what we expect for ourselves and from others.

When mindsets and mottos are overpowering, personal gravity becomes too heavy, making it difficult to move forward or change. Alternatively, if you don't have clear enough guidelines for how to live, you will drift through life without enough personal gravity to hold you in place.

Choosing your mindset

The process of developing mindsets continues all through our lives. Whenever we come to a new situation, we look around to identify the best way to respond. If it works, we then create another mindset to carry us through.

Robin Millar was born with a genetic condition that meant he would lose his sight in early adult life. He had three role models – one of whom allowed his lack of sight to make him different. Robin decided this was exactly what he didn't want. His two uncles on the other hand were powerful people – very masculine, attractive, capable and successful. Blind with style – that's what he wanted – so he developed a mindset that would take him there.

His father helped him develop such an independent mindset by insisting that he learn to box at school: 'You'll get hurt a lot because of your disability, so learn to manage it.' His parents also instilled a real concern for others in the world, so he thinks often of people who are worse off. 'Put yourself in their position and compare – your suffering becomes laughable and it is impossible to feel sorry for yourself.'

An early ambition was to be eminent – to be cool, make money and get women – and his work as a record producer has enabled him to be just that! He travels all over the world with no stick and no dog. It's hard to imagine how it works, but he has learned to break down barriers really quickly with people and finds they are very willing to help. So if an attractive man approaches you in an airport and says 'I know it doesn't look like it, but I can't see a thing and somehow I have to get on my flight to the US, could you help me?' then you might just have met Robin!

You will have mindsets that tell you:

- what a relationship should look like;
- what a relationship should look like;
- what sort of friends you should have;
- what sort of job you are capable of getting;
- what will make you successful in life;
- what is right and wrong.

You know you are hitting a mindset when you say how something *should* be. The *should* and *ought* words are synonymous with mindsets and so worth watching for. And the moment you are totally convinced that you are right about something, that's a sure-fire sign of a mindset!

Do mindsets matter?

Mindsets matter a great deal:

- they can be positive and take you forward;
- they can be negative and hold you back.

And it's up to you which one it is.

Mona, Zena Martin's mother, has always been totally committed to the success of her children. Having completed a PhD in four years alongside full-time work and running a family, Mona knows what it takes to succeed. Her high standards have permeated Zena's life, including the message that she will need to 'work twice as hard to get half as far' because of her colour. As a result Zena has that same grit and determination she saw in her mother and will work hard and persist if she really wants something. She has made the mindset work really well.

Of course, she could have taken it quite a different way. 'If I have to work twice as hard because of how I look, regardless of what I do, then why would I bother!'

Bill also has a PhD, yet he is still determined to hold on to the mindset that he is 'thick'. This is less surprising when you add in underachieving parents who struggled to raise their children. Bill lived his early years with no support or affection and, in the absence of anything to replace it, concluded that he was worthless. Losing his father in early adolescence took away any possibility of turning this around.

Interestingly, he has a brother who is very different. He was only a few years old when their father died, so the effect of poor affirmation and care was reduced. Although also unable to express emotion, he is interested in the world around him and thinks for himself, in an attempt to leave behind all the negative programming. So the mindset still drives him, but in the opposite direction.

Diana Tibble lived for years with the same mindset as Bill – that she was thick. It dated back to the time when she failed the 11+ exam while everyone else in her class passed. However, she has taken the mindset in an entirely different way, spending her whole life working to transcend it. It has taken a long time and been a brilliant spur to action and now finally, after training as a nurse and midwife, counsellor, hypnotherapist and homeopath she is prepared to believe that she is actually quite bright!

So it matters less what the mindset is and more how you take it.

"It matters less what the mindset is and more how you take it."

EXPLORATION

When you respect someone, you give extra weight to what they say. Particularly in early years, you will have listened to a parent and taken their words as absolute truth. This is how mindsets are formed. This exercise is designed to help you identify some of the mindsets you take for granted.

Step one: here we are looking for the statement that you took as an instruction. Write down a list of sentences beginning with:

- I can't . . .
- I should . . .
- I can . . .

Write each one out with three different endings:

Step two: now we need to understand the compelling reason given that you accepted as true, so go through each one and extend the sentence by adding 'because' . . .

For example:

- I should always work hard . . . because that is the only way to succeed.

The final step is to understand the rule you created to ensure you continued to follow the instruction. This is not the initial specific instruction, but the more general behaviour that you have taken on as a rule and applied to a wide range of situations. So go through one more time and extend each sentence again by adding 'therefore' . . .

For example:

- I should always work hard . . . because this is the only way to succeed . . . therefore if I'm not working hard I should feel guilty.

It is this final piece that will give you the mindset. As time has gone by, you will have adapted the mindset and applied it in many ways, yet the essence will remain the same.

Once you have identified your primary mindsets, apply them to your life.

- How do they help you move to where you want to be?
- How do they hold you back?

From this, complete the final column in the table below: do you want to hold on to the mindset because it adds value or realign it to more positive effect?

Mindset/ motto	How it helps	How it holds you back	Hold / realign
I must work hard	Keeps me focused on the work I have to do	Makes it very hard to relax and enjoy myself	Keep the mindset and add in relaxation

Life mottos

Life mottos are a variation on mindsets. They travel with us always and remind us constantly of the life messages our parents/teachers/mentors thought we should have. They give us our life philosophy and impact on values and beliefs – like Peter and his school motto.

Su Lissanevitch has a life motto that has encouraged her in a fascinating life. Her father told her, 'you can do anything you want to' and then both parents did everything they could to help her. So they told her and modelled the behaviour at the same time – a very powerful combination. In her latest adventure she is building and designing ecological earthern houses and gardens in Bulgaria, so I think we can say her father was right!

Andy Wraith's father showed her that 'there are always ways around problems'. Given the family circumstances, providing his daughter with what she needed to achieve in her life wasn't easy. When she asked to play the piano, her Dad offered his skills as a mechanic to the piano teacher in return for lessons. He demonstrated that if you want something enough, there is always a way to make it happen.

In a time of indecision, Andy's willingness to go on the TV programme *Tribal Wives* was just such an approach. All the normal ways of coming to a decision had stopped working – she needed a new way of thinking and what better way to do that than going right out of her comfort zone.

Examples of life mottos:

- You have to work hard for what you want in life.
- Just do it.
- You can do anything yourself, just work it out.
- Don't always listen to others – trust yourself.
- You are bright enough to do better.

These are all positive and have helped their owners make big strides in their lives. We are not all so fortunate, but as with mindsets, it's what you do with the motto that is important, not the motto itself.

EXPLORATION

You can use positive mindsets/mottos in a negative way and negative ones in a positive way – the choice is yours.

Think about the common phrases you heard from parents/teachers that still come easily to your lips. Make a list of them in your notebook and identify:

- how you use it in your life;
- the impact it has – negative or positive;
- how it helps you: does it drive you forward or give you a great excuse not to get on with your life?

Remember that any message can be taken in either a positive or negative way – it's up to you.

Some examples from the people in this book are given in the table below.

Mindset/ motto	Example of how you use it	Impact	Benefit
If you are going to do something, do it well	Lucy making No 1 in the wheelchair tennis world	Drove her to greater efforts	Making the most of a tough situation
I am thick/useless at everything I do	Bill holds back on using his skills/knowledge	Keeps him miserable and negative	Saves him having to challenge himself
There is more than one answer to a problem; it is up to you how you solve it	Harriet getting a first class degree despite dyslexia	Recognised the problem, but refused to see it as a limitation	Challenged any temptation to feel sorry for herself
You won't be able to do that	Barbara sets out to prove she can do it	Gives her a battle to fight	Helps her make the most of herself

Negative use of mottos and mindsets

I guess that the most difficult part of this exercise is seeing how there could possibly be a benefit in following a negative motto or mindset. Yet there must be or why would anyone carry on doing it?

Bill is the example given here. Why would he choose to hold on to a vision of himself as hopeless? Given the total lack of affirmation in his early years, any assumption that he is talented, clever, able feels like a huge risk. Imagine it, no one has ever told you that you are OK – all you get is blank response. So blank becomes the norm. Standing out in any way risks getting back some response – which may be negative – so it is much safer to stay in the shadows and hope no one notices.

Any message that hits us when young, upset or in shock will go in at a really deep level and have a lasting impact. Once this sort of message is embedded, it is hard to shift. So the safest way is to go with it – hence the fact that even following a negative motto can feel like a benefit.

For Bill, buying into the picture of himself as thick, saves him ever taking the risk that he can be proven wrong. He stays within his comfort zone – even though it is such a miserable place – so no one can blame him. If ever he takes the 'test of a life well used' he may be riven with regret at all he has missed, but for now he is content to keep his horns pulled in, rather than face possible ridicule. Looked at from his point of view, that is a benefit.

EXPLORATION

Choose one of your own negative mottos or mindsets and ask yourself: if I didn't follow this rule:

- What risk would I have to take?
- How would I have to see myself?
- What difference might it make to my life?

Consider your answers and decide if you are willing to go for it or whether you prefer to remain where you are.

Take the mindset/motto and consider how you might experiment with proving it wrong, eg:

- I won't believe it.

- I won't give in to it.
- I will ignore it.

Notice how you feel as you think about it in this way – do you feel enlivened, do you feel strong enough to act on it?

Now take the motto/mindset and turn it around to a positive and write it down in your notebook. Once you have done this, take a review of the week ahead and identify opportunities to try out your re-aligned motto and develop some support strategies, as in this table.

Day	Motto: old and new	Established behaviour	First steps in change
Tuesday	Established motto: I am too shy to socialise

Re-aligned motto: I can enjoy socialising | Situation: party at work

Response: won't go – too shy

Feel silly – won't know what to say | Find a supportive person to go with

Prepare possible topics of conversation

Let myself leave when I've had enough |

You will probably feel uncomfortable at first. Change takes time, after all you have carried this motto around for a long time and it is well engrained. But stick with it – at the very least you will feel a sense of achievement that you have started!

"Change takes time … you will feel a sense of achievement that you have started!"

This is just the first step. Keep a diary of what happens so you can look back in a few months and see just how far you have come.

Familiarity

'Of course this is the right way.' 'We always do it that way.' These are killer statements when it comes to change. Taking the familiar option is a perfect example of personal gravity becoming so lightweight that you drift through life without thinking.

Familiarity can also be really positive. It is part of that security that means we don't have to think about the day-to-day practicalities that could so easily distract us from more exciting things.

I'm sure you will think of your own examples. I have certain train/tube journeys I can do without thinking, leaving me free to read the paper. On the other hand, the journey to the station can easily take over, regardless of where I actually want to get to!

The things we take for granted confirm who we are in our lives. I am someone who:

- goes to the gym fairly often;
- likes to see or speak to my daughters, son in law and grandson regularly;
- likes to watch the TV when I'm tired;
- feels shy just before holding a party;
- eats bacon and eggs on Saturday morning with my husband.

They are the things I know and accept about myself. I'm happy with them and miss them when I'm busy elsewhere. As long as I hold them lightly, they provide me with a solid base to work from. If I begin to let them drive my life then they stop being a positive form of gravity and become cast iron boots that don't allow me any flexibility.

Gina Coleman's mother taught her the lesson about flexibility early on in life. 'My mother stopped me one day when she heard me telling a girlfriend I couldn't come out because I needed to wash my hair. She said: 'You know life is too short to wash your hair, you have got to go out.' Gina took that as a life lesson and at the age of thirty-six, had the opposing conversation with her mother, who told her it was no wonder she was so tired, having been out every night of the week!

It is important to recognise the value of familiarity and know the times when it will serve you:

- when you are very tired;
- when you need not to make any more effort and just be with people who understand you;
- when life is all about challenge and you need a rest and some nurturing.

Also, to know the times when it could stop you moving into new territory:

- when you feel lonely and are tempted to stay in rather than make new friends;
- when you feel scared of the new job that could open up an exciting opportunity;
- when you could do the course you've hankered after, but it is on the night of your favourite TV programme.

EXPLORATION

What would your friends or family say:

- You always do.
- You will never do.
- The excuses you give for holding back.

Are they right? If so, decide whether that is helping you make the most of your life or holding you back.

Life pressures

We all have them and they must be given their place among our ambitions, hopes and dreams. It might be the cat, the mortgage, elderly parents, children, money . . . life pressures are the things we can't ignore. We have to find space for then, yet we don't want them to limit us.

In terms of gravity, life pressure goes both ways. When times are tough at home, personal gravity is so heavy we drag ourselves through the day. Yet when life throws us an exciting adventure – like falling in love – we become distinctly lightweight!

Murray Dunlop reached an interesting point in his life. A rising star in the finance industry, he had a dream of being 'the man in the smart suit, with a good car on the drive of a nice family home'. He has done extremely well and at the age of twenty-nine had most of these things already. Then his son came along.

"Time of life will change the pressures."

Suddenly, his priorities changed. He wanted to provide a good life for his family, but finds it difficult having too much time away from his son. For him, pressure comes from the demanding job and his greatest excitement is in being a father.

As this demonstrates, time of life will change the pressures:

- In early adult life, the main pressure will be getting into a job and earning enough money to have a great time.
- Marriage/relationship brings with it pressures around time and competing demands. Serial achievers need support, so this is an important element of success as well as a life pressure.
- If you have children, the focus will change and your ambitions may go on the back-burner for a while.

■ As 'third age' approaches, the pressure is to make sure you will be OK in your senior citizen years. Once this is done, opportunities can open up again – you have only yourself to think about plus the wisdom of the years to carry you through.

Whatever the life pressure, serial achievers give it the priority it deserves. They understand the paradox – attend to the pressure and it won't cause problems, ignore it and it will take time away from the activity that excites you. So Murray made the adjustment, changing his work/life balance in a way that enables him to deliver quality work without detracting too much from his new role of father.

Personal gravity shapes how you live your life and what you believe about yourself and others. It defines what is and what is not possible for you:

■ If your personal gravity is too light, you will feel rootless and adrift in a very confusing world.

■ If too heavy, you will feel restrained and confined.

Keeping your personal gravity in balance is a constant task. The more you learn about the drivers, restrainers and enablers in your own system, the better. Then you can develop a positive gravitational lift that provides you with the agility to take on new options and the confidence to make them work.

Where are you now?

Personal gravity has a very positive part to play in the life of a serial achiever. It is what makes a life familiar and what gives us something to hold on to as we go through change. The trick is in using it well and not allowing it to stop you changing when you need to.

So, now you will:

- understand how your mindsets/mottos serve you well and also hold you back;
- have an idea how to manage your pull into familiarity and how to use it well;
- be clear about your appropriate life pressures and how you want to handle them.

Which leaves you free to consider the life alignment curve: the process of repeating change that serial achievers use so well ...

THIRD FUNDAMENTAL

Harness your life alignment curve

UNDERSTAND THE UNEVEN PATH TO SERIAL ACHIEVEMENT AND WALK IT WITH AWARENESS

When I first met James Nathan he was at a very exciting phase of the life alignment curve. Having recently won the competition MasterChef, he was fresh from the kitchens of a number of Michelin star restaurants and facing the choice as to which one he wanted to work for.

In his early life, the mindset that he needed to please others required him to listen to the parental concern that 'Your friends will be eating the meals and you'll be sweating in the kitchen for no money.' So he did the 'right thing' and trained as a barrister, despite the fact he knew it was wrong from day one. Cooking stayed dear to his heart through a number of life chapters and only lately has he allowed himself to focus on it.

Going at last with his passion for cooking released a huge amount of energy. 'MasterChef is the first time I've ever done something just because I wanted to. And now, for the first time, I am making big decisions on my own without listening to anyone else.' The day we met, James had decided not to choose the restaurant everyone said he should go to, but to go with the one he had really enjoyed working in.

A perfect example of someone who had been held down by his personal gravity, James has found his own voice at last. Coming out of a long incubation period, he is fully focused and ready to go.

What is the life alignment curve?

James set himself up nicely by qualifying as a barrister – plenty of people dream about such an achievement. Yet for him, it wasn't enough. It wasn't the occupation that would leave him feeling satisfied at the end of the day, proud of what he had achieved.

Serial achievers are not thrown by finding they want to do something new or different – this is just grist for the mill. They understand the two basic truths of great achievement:

- What feels right today may not feel right tomorrow – and that is fine.
- There is no limit to the use your can make of your core talent.

The life alignment curve is the process of discovery that enables us to make good use of core talent – through restlessness, incubation and a moment of epiphany, we get into a time of drive that takes us to the peak of success. Once this is completed, then the whole process begins over again, aiming at new heights.

Working as a barrister will have been such a peak in James life – it was a major achievement, his family were rightfully proud of him and he proved that he could focus, learn and succeed. However, it was just the first peak – he didn't believe that was *it* and neither should he – there is a lot more to him yet.

So it is for all serial achievers – they consider themselves 'a work in progress'. We are all entitled to more than one peak in our lives – core talent will take you a lot further than you can imagine. Each peak helps you explore the full extent of your ability, gaining greater understanding of life and relationships as you go. And as you move into each new chapter, you need to re-align yourself and your approach to integrate everything that you have learned and changed, so that you are fully in tune with the next step.

"Each peak helps you explore the full extent of your ability."

The life alignment curve has an upward trajectory overall, leading you to greater and greater heights (Figure 3.1). However, there will be down times along the way and times when you feel you are going nowhere. While you will go up and down through a life chapter, you will certainly end up better off than when you started. And that is just the beginning – don't limit yourself to just one peak – like James, there is a lot more to you yet!

As a serial achiever, you will go through a number of turns of the life alignment curve because:

- you need different things at different stages of your life;
- you have different things to give at different stages of your life;
- you need to use your core talent to its full – this is a human drive that must be addressed.

Attempts to hold back the changes will only leave you locked up and frustrated. Going with the flow and trusting each passage to

Figure 3.1 Life alignment curve

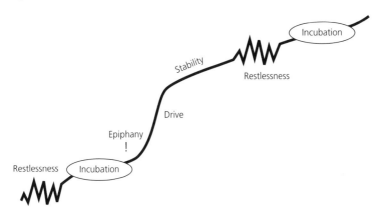

bring you out where you need to be will open up areas of your life that you never thought existed.

Stages of the life alignment curve

Restlessness

As a child, Simon Duffy had an ambition to be Einstein, the archbishop of Canterbury or the prime minister, so he was sure to have a life with plenty of restless moments! He is good at spotting these moments now: 'When my perspective and interests have moved on so radically that I feel I am no longer being really helpful to those around me, I know it's time to change.'

For Dave Pack it is the moment he hits a 'barrier' in his musical development. Now he knows this happens, he sees it as an opportunity to study with teachers, consult colleagues, experiment with alternative approaches or simply spend more time in the practice room.

Su Lissanevitch feels the restlessness first in her feet – she wants to run, jump or dance. Mentally, she just wants the thing she is doing to be over, so she can move on to something new. 'It is when life becomes mechanical, doing the same things over and over again. I love change, so I know I have to keep the challenges coming.'

You will feel restlessness in your own way and, as a serial achiever, you want to spot it as soon as possible. It feels uncomfortable, confusing and sometimes a bit startling. At a surface level the status quo looks pretty good and all is apparently well with the world. Yet underneath, you are itchy, dissatisfied and impatient with the demands your life is making.

EXPLORATION

Look back at the life map you drew in the First Fundamental when exploring your relationship to risk. Review each point where you either took a risk or had the opportunity to take a risk. Think back to how you felt just before the moment arose. Were you:

■ Content on the surface, but concerned that life might be passing you by?

■ Anxious that something wasn't right, you just didn't know what?

■ Itchy and dying to make a change?

Looking back over those times will give you an idea of what restlessness is like for you. The feeling will range from rather unpleasant to extremely exciting depending on your attitude to risk.

Make a note of what this feeling is like:

■ If you are a visual person, you may like to draw a symbol that summarises the feeling for you.

■ If you relate well to music, choose a song that reminds you of restlessness.

■ If words suit you better, write a description of the feeling.

The value of clarifying this feeling is that you will spot it more easily next time, allowing you to take swift action to address your needs.

Acting on restlessness

You may not know what you have to do, just that you have to do something. This is progress – recognising that you are ready for something different. As soon as you can see this, then you automatically move on to the incubation period.

The restless urge is to fly and glide over difficulties to something new and exciting. As an antidote, familiarity and life pressure will attempt to calm you down and show just how risky it will be to change from the status quo.

Both aspects need attention. The truth is you are restless and unless you want to carry on feeling dissatisfied and agitated, something has to change. So do what you need to do to calm yourself and those around you.

- You don't need to rush to action – you can take time to think through the options.
- You should talk to important people in your life to put their minds at rest – help them understand your restlessness and the implications of ignoring it.
- Look to your network and find someone who will listen and understand – maybe someone who has recently come through a restless phase themselves.

Most of all, engage the mindset or motto that will help you make the most of the moment. Remember that there is an exciting time ahead. It may be tough. Equally, it may be fantastic. Whatever happens, you will be better off and you will make better use of your core talent.

Incubation period

The first point in change is to accept it as a necessity. The value of restlessness is that you face up to the fact that what used to work well has stopped being effective.

"What used to work well has stopped being effective."

Some people succeed in pushing that feeling down, so they can carry on as before. Serial achievers, however, use the disturbance to good effect, accepting challenge as the first step towards fulfilment.

The way forward is not always clear, yet the resulting incubation period is always interesting. It is a time of exploration, often spent 'in the dark', seeking a new way forward. It can feel exciting or daunting, depending how you respond to challenge and will link directly to your preferred style of dealing with dissatisfaction:

- introspection;
- investigation.

Introspection

For the serial achiever who defaults to introspection, the first port of call will inevitably be to focus on the feelings. As the dissatisfaction and confusion build, endless questions come to mind:

- Why me? What have I done to deserve this?
- What do I have to do to get out of this?
- How can I possibly move forward against these odds?
- I'm not good enough to cope with it all.
- I don't understand!

It is a time of self assessment – of questioning norms and habits; reviewing past experiences and their effect; looking for answers that will make life more comfortable. It can feel long and arduous. Don't be afraid to ask for help if you need it. Honest friends and supporters can add real value at a time like this or, if you want more anonymity, look for someone who is used to managing change.

If this sounds horribly familiar to you – don't despair. You will come out of it – and with a lot more understanding of how you function and what you can do differently in the future. As long as you stick with it and stay honest with yourself, the penny will finally drop, allowing you to move on to the next stage of growth.

Investigation

The investigative serial achiever will instantly start looking for options and ways forward:

- I just need to ...
- This won't affect me if I ...
- Who can help me?
- I wonder why this has stopped working?
- Let's look at this logically ...

Incubation is the ideal moment to review possibilities. Like Harriet, who could turn her hand to many things, it is important to lay them all out on the table and decide which will provide the security, challenge and fulfilment necessary for success.

Possibilities are endless and it can feel daunting to be faced with making a choice. Fears about getting it wrong, making a fool of yourself, assuming you are better than you are will all raise their heads at some point.

To choose one option means closing down many others, so it is never going to be simple. Once you have some clarity about the future, try out your ideas on a good listening ear. Give real consideration to their response and then make up your own mind. And remember, if you don't get it right first time, the learning gained will help you take the next step.

Brewing ideas

The incubation period is all about brewing ideas, letting them grow and develop until the right moment to take action. To an outside eye, introspectives never seem to come to a conclusion. They discuss possibilities, outlining pros and cons, confounding friends by arguing for and against the same option within a matter of seconds. Investigators seem just to try options in the hope of finding the right one.

In fact, the real decision process is brewing on an intuitive level and when the moment comes, gut reaction kicks in. Like Chris Mullinder who got fed up with his job as a credit controller. 'I don't know why I left, I just wanted something more creative – so I applied for a course spray painting cars.' The idea was to set up his own business, but Chris couldn't find the right premises or get financial backing. While the idea itself didn't work, it did get him out of a rut and was a step on the way to a successful career in sales.

It doesn't really matter how you go about it or what other people think they see from the outside. The ideas will go on brewing whatever happens.

When incubation is the only way forward

Matthew Taylor came to a crisis moment in his life where he had to either keep fighting to sustain his way of working or finally accept who he really was and see where that took him.

After many years in an extremely successful career, he took on a new job as chief executive at the Royal Society of the Arts (RSA), only to find that the challenge was bigger than he had expected. He soon realised that his traditional way of working wasn't going to be effective. It was a difficult and trying time as he struggled to work out what he needed to do differently.

He realised that he had never felt contented or relaxed and had got through life by being a hero – which allowed him to both shine and make mistakes. After all, how could anyone be cross when he was doing such good things? And he *was* doing really good things, so the whole pattern/mindset had been hard for him to spot. 'But now I knew, my style had run out of rope.'

'I had to allow myself to fall into the void, stop using all the devices, cut off the energy supplies to the flawed heroism. I had to create a clearing for something to emerge.'

These are not the easiest of times. Incubation can present a feeling of 'impasse' – as though you have your head right up against a brick wall and there is no way through. Yet, it is actually really fertile. A little like a chrysalis – a great deal of change is going on, but to the outside world it is colourless and utterly uninspiring. And we all know what happens when the chrysalis breaks open – colours are bright and beautiful and life is renewed. Life after incubation is just like that!

"When the chrysalis breaks open colours are bright and beautiful and life is renewed."

Which is exactly what happened for Matthew. Previous success had relied on his core talent of managing challenge and inspiring others. At the RSA, he began to refine that ability with people, learning how to bring them with him in a way that utilised their talents, rather than relying totally on his own. His leadership is improved as a result and he is able to access more of the core talent than was previously available to him.

Managing incubation

First and most important: take the pressure off yourself. It is important to understand that incubation can be interesting and exciting, or very tough. And much of the time you won't be able to take action. The best action is to accept that you are in a time of incubation and that you may need to sit with it for a while. As outlined in Behaviour Two, the moment you accept where you are, change will begin to happen. It is a paradox – the more you try to do something, the harder it will be to move on. I know it will feel counter-intuitive, but, believe me, it's true!

I was working with a client recently who came into the session feeling fed up and helpless. She knew something was wrong, but had no idea what and didn't know how to handle it. She displayed all the classic symptoms of incubation:

- She felt tired and listless.
- She had little or no interest in her work.
- She couldn't be bothered to do jobs at home or to go out to cheer herself up.

As soon as she understood the incubation period and why it was happening, she got some of her energy back. It meant she could stop beating herself up and just work through it in her own time. In fact once she did this, the way was already becoming clearer.

EXPLORATION

If this sounds familiar, take heart – you too are on your way through incubation and the outputs will be very exciting. There are a number of things you can do to help yourself:

- If you are feeling low and exhausted, check out your health, just to be sure it's not something tangible.
- Take the pressure off yourself – this is not the time to do something different or to take major decisions. You are exactly where you need to be.
- Be conscious of what is happening – take time to think about:
    - how you feel and how different situations evoke different feelings
    - what makes you feel frustrated, cross or upset
    - what causes the sun to shine through for a moment

   – who you like to be with

   – the excuses you make for why you are not being successful.

▨ Keep a notebook and look for patterns as they emerge. Track them against the mindsets and mottos you identified in the Second Fundamental, so you know which ones help you and which hold you back.

▨ Don't give in to martyrdom – this is not unique to you. Many people have been through such problems before and come out stronger as a result.

▨ Keep on doing what you are doing and pay attention to how it goes down. Like Matthew, learn all you can about your life pattern and the impact you have: this could be the spur you need for change.

Personal gravity and incubation

Personal gravity drives the way you go through incubation. When you move quickly to epiphany, positive aspects of your gravity have given you the lift and direction. When you feel leaden and stuck, it is your gravity that drags you back.

And personal gravity is what incubation is all about. The reason you are here at all is because something is changing, so trying to move on with exactly the same attitude and approach is unlikely to work. A 'time out' gives you the space to understand what the change is all about and identify the elements of your gravity that will help and those that will be obstructive. You are re-aligning yourself for the next stage of development.

"Trying to move on with exactly the same attitude and approach is unlikely to work."

As you carry on your day-to-day life, huge amounts of activity will be going on out of sight. Just like Matthew, you will be:

- considering where you want to get to and what it needs to look like;

- reinforcing the mottos that support you in making change – like Su with her motto, 'you can do anything you want to do';

- reviewing the mindsets that limit you – like James with his driver to 'please everyone' – and considering how to change it;

- reflecting on your life pressures and analysing which you need to take into account and how;

- checking yourself for attachment to the familiar to ensure you're not holding on for the sake of it.

Think of your personal gravity as an internal driver whose only purpose is to keep you safe. Like Jiminy Cricket in the Disney film of *Pinocchio*, it sits on your shoulder telling you when you are on the right or wrong track.

When you are on the right track, it will spur you on to greater heights, teaching you how to maximise the supportive elements of your gravity. Knowing the positives is a huge spur to serial achievement, so during incubation keep reminding yourself of the mottos and mindsets that reinforce you and your core talent.

When you are going down a blind alley, the beneficial elements of your personal gravity will pull you up and help you re-align for the next step. However, your Jiminy Cricket won't always be to your best advantage – it may also just want you to stay the same and not rock the boat. And the more you challenge the mindset, the more it will attempt to drag you back. Then part of your incubation will be about understanding what drives the negatives and how you can turn them into positives.

EXPLORATION

Think of the negative aspects of personal gravity as an old-fashioned parent with good intentions. The original drive was to keep you safe and, at that time, it would have been the right thing to do. Now you have changed, your needs have changed, so it is time to re-align.

It is tempting to ignore the inner voice and just carry on, but this never really works. Before long you will find yourself back in the old behaviour – and because it is so familiar, it will be a while before you even spot what has happened. You need to understand the original intention and find a way to re-align it to your life now.

- Think of an element of gravity that is holding you back – mindset, motto, familiarity, life pressure – and that you believe is now out of date.

- Think back to a time when the message came into being. You may remember it well. If not, then look for the earliest example of it in your life:
  - Why was it important at the time?
  - How long has it been with you?
  - How strong it is? Rate it on a scale of 1–10.

- Consider how it has served you in your life:
  - Times when it has worked well.
  - Times when you have appreciated the behaviour pattern.
  - How does it serve you now?

- Look at it again and consider:
  - How it holds you back in your life overall.
  - How it is holding you back in this particular life passage.

- Remember the image of gravity as a caring parent – if this was the case, what would you have to do to reassure them that you are fine and that you know what you are doing?

Put all the thoughts together and imagine what this particular bit of gravity would look like, sound like, behave like if it was a separate person to yourself. If you are a visual person, you may like to draw the person. You can give it a name or write a biography as if you were the person. Anything that will help you get a feel for the intention and drive of the force.

Once you have a clear sense of the gravitational drag, make a list of the options for action:

- Understanding and awareness can drive change on its own, so you may already have done it!

- Create a picture of the mindset, motto, etc, in its positive opposite and define how it will help you move forward.

- Adjustments to your behaviour that suit the new style.

Epiphany

The end of the incubation period comes as an epiphany. Such a sudden revelation can arrive at any time and generally involves some good hard thinking about where you are. A moment of deep honesty stops the pretending that everything is fine and opens the way for something real and significant to happen.

For Peter Fisher, it was a car crash that really focused his mind. He had been managing the business he started with his wife – something he had really enjoyed in the early days for the challenge and fulfilment it brought him. 'Then in January 1984 I got hit by a car. It made me realise just how little time I had spent with my kids. So we recruited a managing director and when he was ready to take over, the nanny left and I stayed at home with the children. I stayed as chairman, but otherwise I left the work to others.' He faced up to the fact that he had the balance of life wrong and now the relationship he has with his children is a real source of satisfaction.

Of course, we hope you don't go as far as having a car crash to move yourself out of incubation! There are many other ways it can happen.

For Mark Barnard, it was a moment of real honesty about himself. He looked in the mirror at 4am on a Monday – and he was still drinking. With nowhere of his own to live – he was lodging with a mate – he had hit rock bottom. At that moment, the light went on and he saw himself in all his glory and didn't like what was reflected back at him. That moment of clarity did it all for him – he knew he had to move on – and with that knowledge came the energy and determination that had been lacking for so long. Within a short time, he had a new job, which took him on to building a business of his own.

Epiphany is the result of an incubation spent:

- getting excited about ideas;
- looking for the flaws and why they are a problem;
- deciding that you are just not up to it and it is a crazy idea anyway;
- listening to others who believe they know better – and some who really do know better!
- getting scared about what it would mean to fail – and just as scared about what it would mean to succeed;
- turning your back altogether because the familiar is so comforting;
- getting bored with life and feeling fed up.

It is like the sediment in a wine bottle settling down to a new configuration – it takes time and it is a disconcerting process, but then one day the way ahead suddenly seems obvious.

At the epiphany:

- you will discover that you have endless energy where once you were permanently exhausted;
- you will be fascinated with life, where once you were bored to death;
- you will inspire people with your ideas, where once you were deluged with well meaning advice to give up and stay where you are.

It is *the* most exciting moment. Suddenly the world makes sense, you can see your way forward and you are on your way to a new life chapter.

> "It is *the* most exciting moment ... you are on your way to a new life chapter."

Epiphany is the clarity that results from incubation. It is another paradox – allowing yourself that time to brew and flounder will help the answer drop into place much faster.

Drive

Once you can see the way forward, you will enter into drive. Suddenly you have laser focus. You have masses of energy and enthusiasm for action – you are going full throttle towards something you know is right. That sense of 'rightness' increases commitment tenfold and you become so determined you will not let it drop.

When we really get into gear, life comes up to meet us:

- Things that were a problem become easy.
- People who weren't supportive are convinced.
- Ideas that wouldn't come are ten a penny.

When you are in this phase it seems as if nothing will be a problem again. Be prepared for those around you to be surprised. To their mind, you were in the middle of a struggle, now all of a sudden you are bursting with energy and on your way to somewhere new and different. They can be forgiven for scepticism, so take the time to bring them up to speed with your thinking.

EXPLORATION

You'll know exactly what you need to do in this phase – there is no doubt. However, you can help yourself by continuing to write a journal, paying attention to how you manage and defining your learning along the way. This will give you information for next time round.

Because you will go through this again – even if you have found your lifetime occupation, you still have growing to do and it will be just as interesting next time.

Enjoying stability

As you become familiar with your new direction and settle down into the 'day-to-day' you enter stability. You are becoming good at what you do. You have refined your skills and can manage the challenges that come your way. This is a great feeling, so enjoy yourself – all your learning comes to the fore, allowing you to do really good work.

This is also a time to push the boundaries of your specific area of expertise. Get out into the world and share your learning with others who are on the way up:

- Teach at your local college.
- Mentor a budding serial achiever in your business.
- Offer your services for free to a local charity or community venture.
- Talk to school kids about the work you do.
- Write about your expertise, so others can share your learning.

Look for ways of using your talent and skills in new ways – like Simon Duffy, see what you can do for the common good. Above all, don't underestimate the value you can bring to the world around you. Look around for opportunities that will be of interest.

At some point you may also find that it becomes a bit boring and too easy. But as long as you feel right in your place of stability, it is wonderful – so lap it up! When you are ready, the restlessness will let you know and off you will go again!

Where are you now?

Understanding the life alignment curve is vital to your success. Some places on the curve are frustrating, yet you can't move forward without them. Understanding where you are and why this is happening enables you to go with the process, rather than try and push yourself back into old, less successful patterns of behaviour.

Most important – as a serial achiever, understand that this situation will keep repeating. Whether the outcome of a life chapter is success or failure, nothing is lost. The learning gained will be grist for the mill in the next round of the curve, helping you to develop. In fact, the tough ones are often the most important.

So now you understand:

■ the value of the stages of the life alignment curve;

■ more about the steps you need to take;

■ what helps you move and what holds you back.

All of which gives you a better chance of getting what you want from your life.

So now let's explore what your core talent really is, so you can use it to best effect . . .

FOURTH FUNDAMENTAL

Discover your core talent

LOOK BENEATH YOUR SKILLS TO REVEAL THE CORE TALENT THAT DRIVES THEM

'There are lots of thing I would have loved to do – being a photojournalist for example. The trick was to find what came naturally – what really jazzed me. Why bother fighting the tide!' This is Zena Martin's approach to working with her core talent and it has led her to a really interesting career in communications management. Utilising her strength in building relationships and communication, she is both happy and successful.

As a serial achiever, you also need to find what jazzes you – it is the key to reaching numerous peaks, shining in your life and enjoying your days, knowing that you are adding value to the world around you.

Doing the wrong job or a job you have outgrown is exhausting. It requires you to damp down your energy – you really are fighting the tide. You can't get excited or passionate, so life loses its glow and you lose your sparkle.

What will you do when you grow up?

How many of us really know what we want to do with our lives? From an early age, adults ask little children what they will do when they grow up. Generally, the questioner is looking for a charming answer – the little boy who wants to be a fireman or the little girl who wants to be a nurse or, more probably, a celebrity! Yet just asking puts on pressure. All too soon, a mindset blossoms with the expectation that not only should we *know* what we want to do, but that there is *one* specific answer.

The mindset is cemented by:

- school requiring us to choose a focus early on;
- expectations and hopes of parents;
- our own desire to be grown-up.

Finding a first job used to be the answer that would take you on to bigger and better things – solid bank account, nice home, settled family all leading to a pipe and slippers in later years. Not quite how it works today!

Today, the options are myriad, both in and out of work. The comforting idea of 'pipe and slippers' has gone for good as we change our perceptions of age and growing old.

Core talent just keeps refining

Jill Black has just set up another business in her sixties. Her life has been an adventure from the start to the present day and she shows no signs of slowing down or retiring.

Being the wife of a squadron leader was a job all on its own and one that she took on with gusto. Money was always a challenge in those early days, so she found a range of ways to supplement the income herself, including a design business that made up clothes for kids and then adults, called 'Jill's Frills'.

With a life motto of 'just do it', she believes that each day has to produce something. Just sitting around is a frustration for her, as she focuses on her favourite quote: 'Never let a day slip away.' So retirement is not yet showing up on the radar. Instead, she recently started a garden design business – now she is the boss and her husband is the labourer!

'I wish I had known about garden design earlier, because I love it so much – I love gardens and I love plants. Mind you, as a girlfriend said to me: "If you hadn't done so many different things, you would have less to bring to your garden design." I liked that – it meant I didn't need to regret not doing it sooner.'

This gradual move through to 'different' or 'better' is true for all of us – we build up towards new experiences – nothing is wasted. So feel free to go with what matters to you right now in the knowledge that it will always add something of value, even if you go in a completely different direction later on in life.

"Go with what matters to you right now … it will always add something of value."

For many people, that first job is a bit of a shot in the dark. Barbara Evans went into banking because her mother said that was 'a good thing to do' and chose Barclays because her mother had an account there. Pretty random! However, she did stay with it for eight years and learned a lot while she was there.

EXPLORATION

Reflect on the subjects you chose to study, your training, temporary jobs or permanent employment:

- How did you choose? Was it your choice or driven by someone else?
- Did you know you wanted to go in this direction? When you got there, did you enjoy it?
- How long did you stay and what prompted you to leave?
- What did it teach you – skills, attitudes and behaviour – that will help or have helped with the next challenge?
- What did you learn about what you want to do next in your life?

As you think through these questions, my guess is that you will see that little is wasted. Whatever you do, you take learning forward into the next part of your life. Everything you undertake – studying, holiday jobs, work, self-employment – shows you more of life and helps you define what you do and don't want to do.

The 'one job' syndrome

It has probably always been true that one job can't remain interesting and stimulating for a whole working life, but the tedium and gradual slip into retirement this encouraged was taken for granted.

In fact, we change a little bit from every experience, so each job teaches us something and gets us ready for the next step. What you excel at in your twenties will be very different to what you choose in your forties and fifties.

In addition, the twenty-first century is bringing more change, demanding greater flexibility. We have no idea what is coming. The wise thing to do is to use our talents and gifts to full effect – growing and changing along the way – to ensure we are in good shape when we meet the next challenge.

"Follow your passion and interest."

So give up looking for that one magic job – you would get bored eventually anyway. Instead, look for what you want to offer or have to offer *now* and follow your passion and interest. You will deliver well and store up knowledge and information for use when your next life chapter begins.

It is an exciting prospect for many and a little scary for others. But whoever said we should never be scared! Fear and excitement are close emotions. Often, the only difference is oxygen, as we hold our breath in the face of the unknown.

So breathe deeply and take on the next opportunity with grace – it could be just what you are looking for and will certainly be a great teacher!

What if I don't have a core talent?

If you are alive, you have a core talent. We are all born with something we can do well and that core talent will be available whenever you choose to access it. Even better, you will have more than one – as you refine who you are, you will discover talents that have been waiting for you to be ready.

It is time for us to de-link the word 'talent' from fame and fortune. Yes, TV stars, successful entrepreneurs and atomic physicists are talented. But by associating that talent with glamour, we are being distracted from the simple fact that these people developed skills that made the most of their strengths. And so can you. So let's forget about the glitz and celebrity and look at ordinary people who do their chosen work really well.

- My postman, who has the cheeriest disposition and delivers so many letters and parcels every day without complaint. My guess is that he has the core talent of patience and relating to people.

- Andrew, my colleague, who has a core talent of making the complex simple does a great job helping business clients sort out problems.

- Peter, a computer expert who uses his core talent of seeing patterns and solving problems to keep the machines working.

All these are great people with talents that can be used in other work or occupations if they choose to.

So, as you think about your own core talent, take away that expectation that you need to be better than anyone else or have to make a fortune. You just want to identify the best in yourself, so you can release it and use it really well.

Elements of success

Let's begin by looking at the factors that contribute to success:

- talent;
- skill;
- brain power;
- appetite.

Ask someone to tell you about themselves and what they do well and they will probably tell you about the skills they have. If they don't believe they have skills they will apologise and explain that they are only a housewife, or a shop assistant or . . .

So, what is the difference?

- A talent is innate and always with you. If you don't use it for a long time it may take a while to dust off, but you will still have it. The more you use it, the more refined it becomes. It can also be used in many different situations.
- A skill is something you learn to do by studying or practising alongside experts. When you choose a skill that links to your core talent you will pick it up with ease. Choosing a skill that doesn't link to what you do well makes learning an uphill journey and may mean you never master it.

You will be able to develop your core talent in a range of different jobs, as long as you are interested in developing the relevant skill. For example:

- My postman could use his patience and cheeriness to serve people in a variety of ways – running his home, a steward on a cross-Channel ferry or a school assistant.
- Andrew could use his talent of making the complex simple to teach children, write handbooks for appliances or explain finance to non financial managers.

- The PC expert could use his talent of seeing patterns and solving problems to help locate oil, to predict the weather or help his kids with their homework.

Of course skill development also needs brain power. I can just hear Andrew saying that his mind doesn't work in a financial way – and anyway, he wouldn't enjoy it!

Brain power is the intellectual capacity to understand ideas and put them into action. We all develop mindsets about our ability, prompted mostly by experience at school. Sometimes they are accurate – no one can do everything – but sometimes our assumptions track back to a youthful lack of interest, opportunity or encouragement. The wonderful classic film *Educating Rita* is a lovely example of a person who took the risk of going back to college. Putting in the hard work and determination that eluded her as a schoolgirl, she got a degree and changed her life for the better.

"Life is short, so why spend it doing something pointless?"

Appetite is whether you care enough about something to put in all the effort required for success. We deliver well when the work holds some form of meaning. You don't have to save the world – you just need to care about what you are doing, so the time feels well spent. Life is short, so why spend it doing something pointless?

As you think about your own core talent, take care not to be put off by skills you don't have. Talent endures, while skills are time sensitive. As you refine your ability, so the skills you need will change. As long as you understand your talent and use the brain power available to you, gaining skills will depend only on your appetite.

Understanding core talent

Whatever you have done well and enjoyed in your life to date, your core talent will have been at work. Each time you:

- feel delight in an activity;
- become absorbed and lose track of time;
- can't wait for the next challenge;
- really want to tell someone about your success;
- are full of ideas about what else you can do;

then your core talent is engaged.

Working to that talent feels as if all obstacles have been removed and you are exactly where you are meant to be. It is a great feeling that you will want to repeat over and over.

Don't worry – this won't mean doing the same thing over and over. That's the beauty of core talent – it is fundamental to who you are and lends itself to change and adventure beautifully.

Consider me as an example. I have:

- worked as a biology teacher;
- worked as a social worker;
- been a mum;
- am a wife and a granny;
- had a private psychotherapy practice;
- run a psychotherapy training institute;
- worked as a business consultant;
- set up my own consultancy business;
- become an inspirational speaker;
- written two books before this one.

Where I am now is a long way from those first days teaching the life cycle of the earthworm to fourteen-year-olds. Yet each opportunity helped me refine my core talent of building and understanding relationships.

All my past occupations have relationships at their heart. Some I did better than others – I was certainly too young for my short teaching career – but they all helped me keep refining my original core talent. As that refining took place, so I also uncovered an ability around communication. It is integral to relationships, yet I have been able to focus on it more fully in the last two on the list – speaking and writing.

Core talent zone

When you are working with your core talent, you will experience a feeling of ease and excitement. This is the core talent zone. It doesn't mean there is no challenge or novelty. In fact, there may well be a great deal of both! The range of possibilities you uncover will mean you face:

- new expectations;
- different issues;
- very different people;
- new environment;
- different opportunities.

Yet you know you can do it. There is not that awful panic associated with doing something you know isn't right – the feeling that at any moment someone is going to find you out. You know you are there when you can just drive forward – it feels effortless and quite magical.

Jim Al-Khalili is a theoretical physicist with a core talent of empathy. He loves it when people ask him questions – he goes straight into the groove, putting himself in their shoes to understand what they need to hear. He has friends at home who are not scientists, but are curious about what he does. He loves to talk, 'Shut me up if you can,' and thrives on looking for a way to make it simple. 'I love to see the lights come on. It's as much of a buzz to see them understand as it is to do my research.'

Your core talent

You may know instinctively what your core talent is. It may be exactly what people compliment you on and the very thing you take for granted.

Susan Bull is perfect example of this. She knows her core talent is the ability to see balance and proportion, enabling her to put things in the right place. 'It doesn't have to be perfect. In fact, I don't like things perfect, but it does have to balance.' It fits perfectly with her schoolgirl ambition to dress windows. Now, in her role as a stylist, shop owner and fashionista, this is just what she does: 'Whether in my house, myself, a client, I'm dressing a window. It's visual merchandising.'

However, you may have no idea at all what drives you to succeed. And of course, you may feel that you haven't succeeded yet, in which case you will find it hard to believe that there is talent there at all!

Don't worry, all the information you need is inside you, so you will be able to find out what you are best at and where you need to focus your attention.

Mapping your core talent

What follows is an exercise to help you define your core talent. I have used Murray Dunlop as an example to help you.

Murray has always been fascinated by investments – he loves grappling with the vagaries of the stock market – so his work supporting the finance sector is perfect. With a technology background and an interest in people, he is fast becoming a star in project management. He has also been spotted for his management potential and is now leading his second team. A real high performer, there are numerous opportunities out there for him, but he will make best use of them once he understands his core talent.

Preparation

Before you begin to explore your own core talent, just two suggestions:

- Don't waste time being modest – remember *you have at least one core talent*. You will move on faster if you are honest about your plus points.

- Take time to think through your answers. You don't have to find just one word; better to get the description right.

Step one

When looking at the questions, in Table 4.1, take the first thoughts that come to your mind – this is not meant to be exhaustive! You will probably need to go through it a couple of times before you are sure of your core talent – so give it a go and see where you get to.

Step two

Talk to one or two people who know you really well and ask them to answer the same questions. Use it as an opportunity for discussion:

- Discuss their responses, so you understand fully.

- Put your own point of view and see how they respond.

- Use them as a sounding board for answers you aren't sure about yourself.

Table 4.1 Identifying your natural talents

Question	Pointer	Murray's answer
Name two things you are naturally good at	*This can be anything at all – whether you formally work in this way now or just know you can do it*	Getting on with people Problem solving
What skills have you developed that you do well	*A skill is something you have learned to do* *Identify the skills you have learned that you've carried on using and do well*	Project management Maths, science and technology Playing the guitar Writing
What makes you good at them?	*Look for the underlying reason why you can do these things – it may be driven by a talent or a mindset*	Very determined Able to focus Good at building relationships
What do you do effortlessly that other people respond to?	*What have people said about you directly* *What do they say about you to others*	Listen Ask questions Empathise Challenge, but only when necessary Provide answers and ideas
What do you do effortlessly that you don't see in other people?	*The behaviour, approach, attitude that you believe is normal, yet don't see other people doing*	Seeing a situation from other perspectives

Question	Pointer	Murray's answer
What do other people say you are good at?	*What people admire in you* *What people ask you to do because they know you can help* *If you don't know – go and ask three people close to you*	Being sensitive to others Level-headed Very clear about what I want
What would it be difficult for you to live without	*Assume you have all the practicalities in place – food, home, safety, etc*	Family and security Stimulus and something to work towards
What is your downfall?	*When you behave badly* *The thing that makes you cringe when you look back*	Can get too focused and work too hard
What frustrates you in others?	*What behaviours do you see in others that really irritate you?* *What is it you 'can't believe' about other people?*	Small-minded thinking People who don't see the effect they have on others People who don't listen

Most important of all, take their responses seriously. It may be tempting to push them to one side – please don't do that. Write down the answers and give yourself time to think about it. Remember, this is how another person sees you, so it has to connect to you in some way!

Whatever happens, this will be a very interesting discussion. You will learn a lot about yourself and how the other person sees you – so give time and energy to listening. This is a special opportunity that we don't get very often.

Murray talked through the questions with his wife. It was a really helpful conversation – as they explored the questions, they understood more clearly what drives Murray, so began to think about his work and life in a different way.

Step three

Strong feelings that a particular behaviour is wrong are clues about what matters to you most. What frustrates you in others identifies what you believe to be important in your own behaviour.

Take the answers to the final two questions – from yourself and others you have spoken to – and turn them into a positive. As an example, for Murray, the reframing is as follows:

Negative framing	Positive framing
Can get too focused and overwork	Focus with balance
Small-minded thinking	Be open-minded
People who don't see the effect they have on others	Understand the effect you have on others
People who don't listen	Listen well to other people

Step four

Look at all the answers you have come up with and plot them under the three headings as Murray has done in Figure 4.1:

■ Natural talent: something that comes naturally that you didn't need to learn.

■ Skill: something you have learned to do.

■ Outputs: a tangible outcome of a skill or talent.

Note that you may find some things come naturally to you, while others have to learn how to do them. Always look at yourself specifically: if you have learned something, it is a skill; if it comes naturally to you, it is a talent.

Allocate all your answers to one of the circles, then filter out the ones that are least significant to you.

Step five

Now, look specifically at your natural talents. As demonstrated in Figure 4.1, put crosses or ticks by the talents that link to or

Figure 4.1 Mapping your core talents

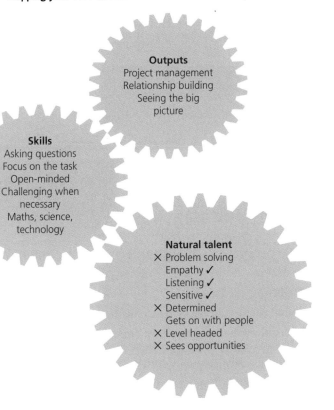

Outputs
Project management
Relationship building
Seeing the big
picture

Skills
Asking questions
Focus on the task
Open-minded
Challenging when
necessary
Maths, science,
technology

Natural talent
✗ Problem solving
Empathy ✓
Listening ✓
Sensitive ✓
✗ Determined
Gets on with people
✗ Level headed
✗ Sees opportunities

support each other. Once this is clear, write them out again into separate groups by the linkages. As you look at the groups, decide which talent is the overarching one, ie, the talent that is served by others, rather than serves others – this is the core talent.

From Murray's example, you can see that grouping the natural talents together (✗ / ✓) leads to two areas:

- Problem solving which is supported by his determination, level-headed approach and his ability to see the wider picture.

- Getting on with people, which links with empathy, being sensitive and able to listen well to others.

This suggests that his core talent is getting on with people and problem solving.

Step six

Join up your core talent and skills/outcomes so you can see:

- how your core talent support your skills;

- how your core talent deliver the outputs you see in your daily life.

In terms of skills, to refine his core talent of getting on with people, Murray has honed the skill of asking questions and keeping an open mind. When combined with his skills of challenging appropriately and focusing on the task at hand, they also enable his core talent of problem solving.

As for outputs, the core talent of problem solving makes Murray an ideal person for project management. Coupled with his talent for getting on with people, he is able to build the strong and robust relationships that mean people will support him and deliver the necessary work in time.

Murray is clearly well suited to his present line of work. However, with these core talents, it is possible to see a variety of options for the future. This is the beauty of focusing on a core talent rather than skill – it helps you open up brand new possibilities!

Findings

Don't expect to get your core talent exactly right first time. The main value of this exercise is to start you thinking in a different way. You will end up with a first pass and I suggest you work with this to see how it settles. Once you start to think about these questions, your mind will become attuned and you will spot other things you are good at.

"Don't expect to get your core talent right first time."

So mull over this first finding and revisit the exercise after a couple of weeks to see if you come up with something different or, more likely, a refinement of what you find this time.

Making the most of core talent

Using the motto her father gave her – 'you can do anything you want to do' – Su Lissanevitch has used her core talent in many ways in her life. She is brilliant at demystifying the things that rule our lives and the different challenges she has faced helped her hone that talent into a fine art.

Early in life, she taught English in Kathmandu with Voluntary Service Overseas (VSO). Part of her learning at this time was seeing the depth and ability demonstrated by the women there. She is seeing the same now as she works in Bulgaria. It confirmed her belief that we can do anything if we want to.

She stayed in Nepal after marrying, so when her first child had a serious illness she came into contact with Ayurveda, the traditional form of

Indian medicine. She was so impressed with the results that she set about training with the best teacher she could find. She wanted to demystify the process for herself and others, disliking the patient passivity of western medicine.

She didn't stop there. Always on the search for ways of helping her son, she went on to train and practise aromatherapy and Bowen – alternative healing therapies that she passionately believes in. Armed with these skills, she then wanted to help others, so became a teacher and trainer in both disciplines.

Now that her son is a healthy adult, she can move on to a different arena, so is focusing her attention on building eco-homes. Living and working in Bulgaria, she has taken on renovating a traditionally built home and also building a straw bale house in the garden. And, of course, she will run courses to teach others how to do the same!

She is determined to demystify again. 'If a woman wants to build her own home, then she can do – she just has to work it out.' And to prove the point to her doubting builders in Bulgaria, she is building a cob house (made with mud bricks) in the garden for her guests, while they work on the main home.

So her core talent leads her to think things through and work out what needs to happen. And thanks to the motto from her father plus the life experiences, she is using it really well.

Core talent and life

Your core talent will serve you in all areas of your life – work is just one aspect. Once you have worked out your talent, think about ideas you have had in the past for hobbies and pastimes, but never got round to. Now you know you have the talent, you can get out there and give them a go.

Andy Wraith took up sword-fencing to widen her horizons and learned a lot from the experience. 'I realised how important it was to have a rough plan, but then relax into the game, so I could react to the unexpected.' She took this understanding into her life: 'Plan ahead and acquire the skills, but don't be strait-jacketed – leave yourself emotionally and mentally supple, so you can take opportunities as they arise.'

Gina Coleman took on a voluntary role as a trustee of a local cancer hospice. It was work that mattered to her because of family history and was a great place to put into practice her core talent for building relationships and helping people. Her ability meant she developed a fabulous network of people who could provide support and she became a friendly face that everyone appreciated.

So take a good wide look at your life for ways of using your core talent:

- sports;
- community involvement;
- creative outlets – painting, gardening, amateur dramatics;
- holidays;
- voluntary work.

Keep in mind that when you use your core talent, it feels easy. You are in the right place at the right time, doing exactly what you need to do. It's a great feeling, so use every opportunity to enjoy it.

Values

Values underpin your core talent and are just as important. You will achieve most by working with them hand in hand, since they drive both what you are good at and what you are happy to do.

Values are key to everything we do and often only come into consciousness when threatened. They are also inextricably linked to core talent, determining how we are prepared to act, so how we can use the talent that we have.

Zena Martin is very clear that she can't work just for money – her time has to be worth more than that. She uses her core talent of relationship building and communication to help organisations become fully engaged in diversity, so they dovetail well with all of their employees and customers. This is something dear to her heart: 'We only have one life, so need to grab it with both hands.' She won't sit back and see people limited because of their colour, gender, age or disability. This is about her values of being transparent, honest and fair, so is something she really believes in.

Work is always more powerful when it aligns to values. It stops being just a way to fill the fridge and becomes something that has meaning.

Values also serve another purpose: They help us identify the right battle or challenge to take on.

When we are faced with a difficult choice, we consider it in two ways:

First, by thinking it through rationally:

- the impact each choice will make on our livelihood;
- how much we want or don't want each option;
- what others will think about us;
- whether the different options open up possibilities in the future;
- which option we will enjoy most.

This thought process provides a great deal of information and helps form a mental picture of what the options are. Sometimes, this will be enough for the answer to pop up.

Secondly, if that is not enough to clarify, we consider our values:

- What is the right thing to do?
- What will be the impact on other people?
- Would we be proud to speak of it to others?

When the dilemma is a tough one, the rational review will never be enough on its own. We always need to balance the options against our values. Ignoring values can leave you feeling as if you are pushing upstream – the complete opposite of the flow that goes with using your core talent.

"Ignoring values can leave you feeling as if you are pushing upstream."

Values provide you with the perfect measure. As Simon Duffy says: 'It is sometimes important to avoid over-thinking the risks and just do the right thing.' The 'right thing' for you is determined by your values. When you do this, tough decisions make themselves, based on the deliberation:

If I take this action:

- Can I live with myself?
- Will I be able to look others in the eye?
- Am I being true to myself?

Answering these questions will help you decide which challenges you need or want to take on and which are beyond your boundary. As long as you can answer a resounding 'Yes' then you are being true to your values. If the answer is 'No', put the idea on one side and move on.

Defining your values

We all know instictively, what our values are, yet we rarely take the time to define them in words. However, it can be helpful to have a rational understanding when tough decisions need to be made. To know why you behave as you do can be reassuring and makes it much easier to explain your actions to other people.

EXPLORATION

Step one

It is not always easy to put words to values. One way to begin is to think through the things that really upset you. So complete these sentences twice each:

- I get upset when people . . .
- I hate it when people . . .
- I dislike it when the following happens . . .

This will put you in the realm of values and give you an idea of the behaviours/attitudes that matter to you.

Step two

- Fill in the left-hand column of the table opposite to identify the expectations you place on yourself and others.
- Then address the middle column: how do these expectations influence your day-to-day behaviour? How do you live out your expectations?
- From these two explorations you can take a first pass at defining your values – the themes you hold dear in your life and that you are not prepared to give up on.

Expectation	How I act on this in my life	My value is ...
People should ... *do as they would be done by*	*Treat others as I would want to be treated*	*Be respectful of others*
What matters most to me is ... *the wellbeing of my family*	*Be there when the family need me* *Build strong family ties*	*Look after each other*
What I care about most is ... *the dignity of people*	*Help businesses create great workplaces for employees* *Coach people to use their talent well*	*Be the best you can and lead a valuable life*
I won't tolerate ... *dishonesty and disrespect*	*Maintain honest relationships* *Challenge poor behaviour*	*Be respectful*
I feel angry when ... *people are not trustworthy or behave badly*	*Speak out* *Challenge the behaviour*	*Be trustworthy and respectful*

As you can see from the exploration, the values begin to repeat as you go through the exercise. You may need to work it through a few times before you get the full range of your values.

Hierarchy of values

How we interpret values will vary. When life is going well, we can be expansive and reach out in a wide circle to the world around us. When life gets tough, the circle contracts:

- Good times action: this is the way we interpret values when life is going well. For example, a value of caring for others will drive you to help someone you see on the street who is homeless and needs food. When your own life is expansive and comfortable, you can interpret your values generously and apply them to a world that is in need.

- Challenging times action: when life becomes a challenge, then it is easy to reduce the reach of the circle and focus on self, family and friends. If you have a value of caring for others, a challenge will focus your mind on those who form the centre of your life – you will have little free attention left for those outside. You will look after family and close friends first. This is how we preserve the world as we know it.

- Crisis action: when life gets really tough, then we are more likely to widen out our circle, because we recognise that we can't manage a major crisis on our own. So in times of tragedy or struggle, people pull together and apply their values to those around them as well as their family, knowing that mutual support and care from all sides is more likely to get us through. So after the world wars and such events as 9/11 and 7/7 people stepped in to care for strangers as they would care for their own family.

So as you look at your values, be aware of these differences. It will help you define them more easily without being too tough on yourself.

Values and core talent

Once you link your values with your core talent, decisions suddenly look different. Knowing what you do well and what matters to you means you can tell instantly whether a job or pastime is right.

Laura Pelling finds it very hard to fail – it really challenges how she sees herself. Yet she also knows that the biggest failure of all is to behave in a way that is outside her values. Top of the list is to care for her family, something she was tested on in a previous job. Given her part-time status, when the company went up for a management buyout, she knew she would be allocated fewer shares than full-time employees. There was an option to go back full-time, which would have made the family a great deal richer, but that would have lost her time with her kids when they were little. 'I always think of family first, and then about my personal integrity. I want to feel comfortable in my skin – to feel good about what I'm doing and how I'm doing it.'

Sticking to her values is the only way that Laura can 'feel comfortable in her skin'. It's a good description – bear it in mind as you think of your own values. Living in harmony with your values will make a real contribution to the test of a life well used.

Where are you now?

As you become clear about your core talent and your values, you will understand:

- that there is more to life than just one job;
- that everything you do provides learning and experience for the future;
- the skills you have developed to date and those you need to focus on now;
- the values that form the basis of who you are.

With all this information you can move on to the next step – understanding what you need to be successful ...

FIFTH FUNDAMENTAL

Address your needs

SECURE SUPPORT, SEEK OUT CHALLENGE AND HAVE THE COURAGE TO BE HONEST

'The perfect situation for me is working to the very best of my ability– stretching to my limits. When I can do that with good people and feel appreciated for doing it – that is wonderful.' This is Chris Mullinder's ideal work setting.

Taking time to understand what you want from life is a really important part of being successful. That means focusing on you – your core talent, your personal needs and the passions that drive you forward.

In my book, *Inspirational Manager*, I clarify that managers need to balance the time they give themselves with the time they give to others. This is equally important for serial achievers. To do fantastic work, you need to feel strong and positive about yourself. Then other people will want to include you in adventures because of the difference, excitement and energy you bring.

So before you rush into your next activity, give some thought to your own needs – the needs that will help you make the very best of your core talent.

The three needs

Three needs are central to success:

- courage and deep honesty;
- backup and support;
- ongoing stimulus and challenge.

Addressing all three gives you the foundation from which to go from strength to strength in your life. Miss out on one of them and your way forward will feel sticky and difficult.

Courage and deep honesty

It is easy to look at serial achievers and consider them courageous for what they have accomplished. In fact, what looks like courage from the outside is rarely how it feels on the inside. However, the moments of facing up to self – those difficult times in incubation that call for searing honesty – require real nerve.

Facing the demons

Tunde Banjoko found it really hard when his mother died suddenly of a heart attack. She had been highly significant in his life – a constant source of encouragement as he worked on building a home for his family and a place of support for the unemployed. Yet the fact that she had been such an appreciative mother left him feeling a fraud – he just didn't think he had done enough. The only way Tunde could cope with it all was to carry on doing what had made her proud.

Being awarded an OBE just added to his misery because she wasn't there to enjoy it with him. She had worked so hard for him to be successful, so he accepted it as a thank you to her. Yet, despite it all, he still felt a failure.

A conversation with a millionaire he met on holiday brought him to an epiphany. He realised that his mind was set on a success defined solely by financial security, something he had little energy for. The work that really excited him was helping people – and his time at LEAP showed that he was already a success in that!

Looked at in this way, he could see why his mother was so proud. She always went out of her way to help people, so really appreciated the great work he was doing. For the first time, he felt proud too, so he could carry on and make even more of his strengths. Tunde's courage was less in what he achieved and more in that moment of deep honesty, when he accepted that his definition of success didn't work for him.

In practice, he had been working to his strengths and core talent all along – he just couldn't see the value he was adding, because of his mindset. As soon as he was honest, his mood changed and all that energy and focus returned to enable him to take action.

Once you see the truth, the way really does open out. The problem is not in moving forward, it is in understanding what holds you back. Once you know what is happening, the next steps become much easier.

"The problem is not in moving forward, it is in understanding what holds you back."

Key areas for honesty

Being completely honest about what drives you is essential if you want to:

- understand your core talent, even if it is not what you thought it would be;
- address the relationships that help and/or hinder you;
- accept that you make mistakes and are not perfect;
- value your talents and skills without waiting for others to tell you.

To understand your core talent sounds as if it should be an easy one – except if you have assumed it was something different. Miriam McLoughlin always knew she wanted to go on the stage and everything about her was working towards that aim. Yet when she got to college it became clear that she wasn't in sync with the culture and ethos of the profession. She experienced a two-year incubation period, while she tried every possible way to align herself. Finally, she came to a moment of deepest honesty – her dream was never going to make her happy. It was a dreadful moment of facing the void – if not this, then what?

There is an important pattern to deep honesty – facing up to the worst is tough, but it is also a release:

■ once you take the pressure off trying to be something you are not, there is the chance to be who you really are;

■ by being open to the problems, you also open yourself to solutions.

Shortly after her darkest moment, Miriam realised what joy she took in seeing others succeed. She realised that being an actor's agent or casting director would give her the opportunity to be part of the creative aspects of the work without having to sit in a culture that went against her own values. It would also make best use of her core talent of encouraging, supporting and enabling others.

Courageous deliberation

When a serious choice faces you, it is important to look at it from all angles. Only then will you have a real understanding of the impact on your life, what will be demanded of you and whether you are willing to undertake the challenge. This is a process that requires real honesty as you progress through the five steps of deliberation:

1. Define the issue.

2. Reflect on the impact it makes in your life.

3. Review against serial achievement.

4. Revisit the issue.

5. Make a plan.

EXPLORATION

Let's follow Miriam through the process as an example.

Step one

Define the issue as you presently understand it: write a short description of the opportunity or problem to be considered.

Miriam was given the role of assistant director for a play. It required her to support the director and the cast, turning her hand to whatever was needed at the time. Given the recognition that her dream wouldn't make her happy, she questioned whether this sort of work might be suited to her core talent.

Step two

Review the issue in terms of how it impacts on family, work, relationships, your commitment and the opportunities offered. Use Figure 5.1 as a guide for the different elements, adding in any that are specific to you.

Miriam is excited by how much she is learning from the experience. Of course, it is tiring, but very rewarding when she gets it right. Because it is a short-lived project, there are no downsides with regard to family and it may even lead to new friendships.

Step three

Use the deliberation table (Table 5.1) as a framework for assessment. This will show whether you are presently able to drive forward or whether this is a time for restraining yourself.

First, two definitions:

When you are *driving forward*, you feel:

■ positive and interested in life;

■ energy for the challenges that face you;

■ excited about what is coming next.

In this case, your satisfaction level will be high.

When you are *restrained*, you feel:

■ lethargic and lazy;

■ stressed and confused;

■ disinterested in life.

In this case, your satisfaction level will be low.

The purpose of the deliberation table is to enable you to review what helps you move forward and what might be holding you back as you face an issue. To do this well requires courage and deep honesty as you take a good look at your patterns of behaviour.

To determine your satisfaction rating, look at what your list of what helps and what holds you back and see which is most dominant right now. Then give yourself a score: 10 = you are moving forward positively; 1= you have the brakes well and truly on.

Figure 5.1 Deep honesty

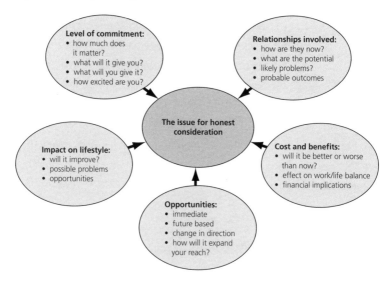

Once you have the final numerical output, you will see exactly where you need to focus or change the way you behave, giving you a much greater chance of success.

For Miriam, the table reads as in Table 5.1.

Table 5.1   Miriam's deliberation table

	What helps you	What holds you back	Satisfaction rating 1–10
Core talent: *Enabling others*	*It is satisfying to see the actors shine in a good production*	*Can do too much for others and forget herself*	5/10
Mindsets 1. *I won't be able to do it!* 2. 3.	*Won't take on something if she thinks she can't do it, so is fully committed when she says 'yes'*	*If she starts to worry, goes into panic and wants to give up*	7/10
Personal motto 1. *It is important to appreciate people who help* 2.	*She likes being appreciated, so will work hard for people around her*	*She gets angry when they don't see how much she has done for them*	6/10
Managing dissatisfaction: ▪ **Introspective** ▪ **Investigates** ✓	*Talks to people to find better options*	*Gets frustrated when there is too much complexity*	9/10
Total			27/40

Analysing the result leads to the following conclusions:

- This work uses Miriam's core talent of encouraging, supporting and enabling others. She enjoys the thrill of creating something of quality and likes to see the actors thrive. But she can easily put in too much effort and end up feeling undervalued. At present she is working a bit too hard, so scores 5/10.

- Her mindset leads her to doubt herself. As long as she is conscious of this, it keeps her focused on the task. If she starts to worry, then she is likely to work so hard to get it right that she wears herself out. Right now she is feeling pretty strong, so scores 7/10.

- When it comes to her life motto, Miriam has always believed that it is important to appreciate people who make a real effort. Since she also likes appreciation herself, she will work hard to do a good job. However, she struggles when people fail to see what she has done – even though she won't tell them. As the production approaches and others are more demanding, her frustration levels are rising, so 6/10.

- Managing dissatisfaction: Miriam is investigative, so keeps looking for plans and options that will help her move through a tough time. It serves her well in this situation, although can stop her accepting the 'good enough' option when under pressure. At present she is being very creative, so 9/10.

Her total is 27/40, which indicates the job will suit her core talent, but she will need to watch for overworking – her desire to be appreciated could lead her to exhaustion.

Step four

Revisit the issue. Once you have completed the exercise, go back to the original issue and see if it still looks the same. You may find that you need to redefine it as a result of your thinking.

As an example, Miriam can now see that looking for appreciation is a risk to her success. Better to do a good job just for the sake of the production and value *herself* for how hard she has worked. Doing this takes away the risk of overwork and frustration at the attitude of others.

Step five

Create a plan of action to address the real issue. Before you make a decision or take a step, sleep on your findings. You may find that further ideas present themselves and help to clarify the next steps.

For example, Miriam reviewed her day and focused on the production, allowing others to do their job. The end result was a great production and lots of appreciation for everyone.

Whatever you come up with, remember that every situation holds potential and it is often the most challenging times that help us move forward and out of an old restraining rut.

Fear and dreams

Having a dream is wonderful, very exciting – and passive. Taking action requires you to let that dream come up against your fear of failure. This is *the* moment of courage and deep honesty. It can be pretty scary, but until you do, you can't move anywhere.

The moment where fear and dream collide comes when:

- You make a statement to the world about what you are going to do or who you are. While you hug your idea to yourself, there can be no repercussion – you are in total control. As soon as you include others, you relinquish control and lay out your ideas, beliefs or activities for their judgement. Then if you fail, everyone will know.

- You try out an idea that in theory should work well. Putting the theory into action means that you face the fact that it might not work. What was a wonderful dream may be a poor reality.

If you feel that you are not progressing towards achieving your dream, you need to sit down and honestly consider what elements of your own attitudes and behaviours are blocking your path. This is scary because, in the light of that consideration you will have two choices:

- address those attitudes and behaviours;

- accept that you will continue to be limited and that your acceptance of them will damage your chance of ever achieving that dream.

Letting fear and dream collide

Zena Martin faced the fear/dream moment when she decided to go to boarding school. Her parents backed her, believing she would learn from the experience. They were right on a number of fronts. The day-to-day reality of her decision wasn't quite what she expected. When she asked to go home, her parents held her to her choice – she had made her bed!

'I felt sick to my stomach. I just wanted to hide under my duvet or crawl under a rock. I had gone from being a big fish at my private day school to a little fish in an unfamiliar pond, without my friends. I didn't always make the first team – I just wasn't so fabulous here!'

'I soon realised that it was OK to feel like that, but not to stay like that. I sat with my misery for a bit, then took a deep breath and got on with it.' It wasn't all plain sailing for Zena. She did fail in some areas, yet learned a good lesson and created a life motto for herself: 'If you've done the best you can and it hasn't worked, then it wasn't meant to happen, but some good will always come of it.'

The benefit for Zena was finding that she was a lot stronger than she thought she was – learning that stood her in good stead when she moved to London. Just like going to school, she moved to a different pond with no friends and just had to make her way. She tried new things and they didn't always work, so she persisted with some and let others brew for a while. Sometimes she thought it was just too hard and wondered why she was putting herself through it, yet knew she didn't want to give up.

The 'deep breath' moment

Zena has had many a 'deep breath' moment when she just needed to jump right into the deep end. Just as you will when entering into a time of deep honesty – and it will be worth it as you gain in personal strength. You will:

- know more clearly what you want;
- understand that what happens is up to you;
- recognise that you can choose one behaviour over another;
- face real choices that can improve your life;
- have the chance to give up your negative, life-draining behaviours.

So take a deep breath and off you go.

Put to one side the temptation to judge – everything you do, you do for a reason, so there is no point in blaming yourself. It is just another opportunity to review the outputs and decide if you are acting for the right reasons. Whatever happens, you will learn more, maturing yourself and your core talent.

Of course, you may not take a deep breath. Instead, you will be full of reasons why not to take the plunge. Observe yourself in avoidance – just pay attention and you will gain worthwhile information. If you sidestep yourself now, you will also be doing it in other areas of your life – so you have a real learning moment at your disposal.

Remember that the willingness to be deeply honest is the hall-mark of serial achievers. The courage to look in the mirror with clear vision is the key to navigating the incubation period and coming out the other side. In contrast, a familiar rut acts as a great anaesthetic – it numbs frustration and passes the responsibility on to someone else. It works fine if that is what you want. If you want more, then it is back to honest delibera-tion – there is no real replacement.

"A familiar rut acts as a great anaesthetic – it numbs frustration and passes the responsibility on to someone else."

Backup and support

After winning MasterChef, James Nathan spent time in the kitchens of the prestigious restaurant, The Vineyard. This was one of a number of places that had offered him a job and he was having a hard time deciding what to do. The chef, John Campbell, was extremely helpful and made a huge impression on him. A self-made Liverpudlian with the gift of the gab, he confounded James by asking him how he would get to Dumfries. 'So James said: 'I'd get a map.' 'Exactly,' replied John. 'Once you have a destination you can make a route. Think first about where you want to get to.'

For James, this was really helpful. His mindset about pleasing other people means that he can easily put his own ambitions on the back-burner. John's comment gave him the permission to decide his own direction, instead of waiting for others to set it for him.

We all need people who tell us home truths and who will guide us for our sake, rather than their own. When we find them, they become very special. They will be:

■ understanding and accepting;

■ generous in putting their own needs on one side to help us;

■ demand that we are honest and respect ourselves.

Positive backup

Chris Mullinder has been fortunate to have two big supporters in his life. He and his sister Margaret have been through difficult times together, providing backup and a listening ear for each other when needed. And without his wife, Cath, he isn't sure that he would ever have taken the plunge to change his career so dramatically from sales to childcare. 'We worked out that we could just about manage on her wage and whatever money I could bring in. Not only did she support me financially, she was willing to accept a reduced income overall to give me the chance.'

As Susan Bull opened her second fashion shop she also knew she couldn't have done it without her husband, Kelvin. He provided a sounding board as she built her reputation, experience and expertise as a stylist. Keeping the books, helping with shop design, even shifting boxes of stunning clothes, he was always there in the background.

Yet, providing that support is not all Cath and Kelvin do. They also ask the tough questions and challenge thinking. It is no support to just go along regardless, watching as ideas fail and money is lost.

Every serial achiever needs a robust, critical friend. Someone who will always speak the truth as they understand it. Of course, they won't always be right, but at least they get you thinking and reviewing to make sure you are going the best way around something.

A backup and support person can be a:

■ partner;

■ close friend;

■ mentor or coach;

■ parent or sibling;

■ teacher.

The most important factor is that you trust the person to have your best interests at heart and that you don't feel you have to

THE PSYCHOLOGY OF SUCCESS

please them. As soon as you agree, rather than take the risk that they will be offended, then the critical friend element of the relationship is lost.

The value of positive support

The trauma of losing her sister caused Harriet Kelsall to re-evaluate what she wanted in her life. She decided:

- Life is too short to waste it.
- If I'm going to do something, then I have to give it a proper try.
- I need to find out what I want to do and get on with it!

Her vision of the future was pretty cloudy – as a talented young woman, there was a lot she could have done. It was when she met Tim that things became clearer. He was very supportive of her jewellery-making and encouraged her to explore the possibilities.

Her father had made jewellery as a hobby, so she had grown up watching him at work. They converted the garden shed into a workshop and she began making rings – just like her father before her. It was demanding alongside a full-time job, but then Harriet likes to be busy and involved with lots of different things.

As the commissions began building up, Tim encouraged her to give up work for a year and focus on this. 'I saw her as already successful – she just took the leap a bit sooner with my backup.'

Negative support

While the intention might be good, some people will offer 'support' that is in fact unproductive. Tim was great for Harriet, but her mother had real trouble being positive and felt she had to speak her mind. In the end, Harriet had to stop listening because it was just too debilitating.

This is a tough one, because it is really important not to bat away a robust challenge – if you can't listen to the concerns of those around you, then you may miss something of real importance. So how do you know the difference between a good quality critical friend and a detractor?

A critical friend will:

- want you to succeed;
- be willing to see the world through your eyes;
- won't push for their own way;
- be open to new ideas and review their own thoughts/concerns;
- be pleased to say when they have been wrong.

A detractor will:

- want to control you;
- have a clear picture of where they want you to be, regardless of what you want;
- be a poor listener;
- be unwilling to change their view of life;
- continue to put forward their concerns even when you are successful.

Interestingly, the intention may well be the same – both supporters will want to see you succeed and have a good life. The difference is in the mindset. A detractor will have less faith in your judgement than their own, so they genuinely believe that you will be better off following their advice. They are also more likely to be cautious as they try to protect you from yourself.

This is an easy trap for parents to fall into, because they do have more life experience and may well see more clearly. Hence so many people who go first into the job their parents want them to have. Like James who went into law, when all he really wanted to do was cook.

And it's not only at the first stages of work life – some parents carry on 'knowing better' for a very long time!

When the parent/young adult relationship becomes unproductive, it is always a joint venture:

▪ Parents want the best for their offspring. They have a view of what they might do well and what will enable them to live a good life. They also have electricity bills and mortgages in mind, as well as an interesting job. They definitely believe they know their child well.

▪ The young adult loves their parents, so either has to go along with it or fight hard as a way of gaining escape velocity. The last thing they care about is bills and mortgage; they just want to get going. Not sure yet who they are – they are a work in progress – they just want to explore the options.

It is a tough one – elders may well have good information and experience to share, but also need to accept that mistakes have to be made and that they might just have to sit back and watch.

"The serial achiever won't always please other people as they move ahead."

The serial achiever needs to listen and evaluate any advice, ideas and concerns before deciding which are important. They also need to accept that they won't always please other people as they move ahead.

Recognising the joint responsibility can help you effect change. All you have to do is change the way you respond and the other person will have to change too, since the old pattern won't work any more.

EXPLORATION

Think about the people who currently offer you support and advice. Fill in one column for each person, scoring each statement on a scale of 1–10 (very positive = 10; very negative = 1). This will help you clarify their approach and identify who can give you the backup and support you need.

Name:				
Relationship				
Intention: *are they in this friendship for you both (positive) or just themselves (negative)*				
Understands you				
Willingness to listen				
Open to new ideas				
Enjoy your success				
You feel you can say no				
Helps when you get it wrong				
Doesn't blame				
Total out of 80				

If you allocate high score in all factors then you have a very good support system.

If you have a good friend who is not good on some of these things, there are two things to consider:

■ What sort of support or friend are you to them? We receive as we give, so if your friend feels you don't listen and that you just want to have your own way, then why would they bend over backwards for you?

■ How honest are you being? If you choose to go along with them rather than risk hurting them, then you are contributing to a one-way relationship. Give some thought to how you might ask for a different type of support so that the relationship is more productive and useful to you both.

Ongoing stimulus and challenge

It is in the nature of serial achievers to enjoy a good challenge! The greatest risk is boredom – the feeling of not moving forward or learning. They may not define it in this way, but they will be quick to pick up monotony and the desire for stimulus.

It comes from that understanding that we have just one life, which is remarkably short. So why waste it? Remember Jill Black and her motto, 'Don't let a day slip away.' It is all about enjoyment, being excited and having something that demands you use your mind and make the most of yourself.

Life challenges

For some people, the challenges come at them from life, demanding that they sort themselves out. For Naaz, that moment came early when she didn't do well at A-level. 'It shook me because I was a real achiever. If I came fourth in the class, it was shedding-tears time. It helped me realise that A-level exams required me to reason and think more, rather than just survive on good memory. I went from Tanzania to England to do my degree and there was no question about me not doing well. It was total focus and I came out with a first class honours.'

Naaz wanted to be the best and youngest chief pharmacist and was determined that she would do well. She didn't let any other possibility enter her mind. It set a standard, encouraging her to take on other challenges as they arose. Like the day a letter landed on her desk asking if she would consider being chair of the British Refugee Council. Having only worked with refugee doctors and some refugees from Uganda when they came to the UK, she didn't feel she had the right experience. However, her chief executive encouraged her, saying: 'You will learn it.' So she went for it and got it.

"Although demanding and a bit scary, challenges are enlivening."

Although demanding and a bit scary, challenges like this are enlivening. Lack of challenge leads to:

- loss of energy;
- boredom;
- low self esteem;
- lethargy;
- lack of purpose.

It comes back to that old adage. 'If you don't use it, you'll lose it.'

A true challenge is something that:

- you have never done before in this particular way;
- is not presently in your skill set;

- requires you to grow your knowledge;
- is stretching and demanding;
- piques your excitement and interest.

For a challenge to catch your imagination it also needs to mean something to you and fit your core talent.

In essence – you will be excited and a bit scared, yet know that the task is within the realms of your ability.

Self-imposed challenge

Some people set out to create the next challenge, rather than continue with a job or lifestyle that they know is no longer right.

Taking the plunge

Mark is a perfect example of someone who chooses a challenge. After the epiphany that showed him the full impact of his lifestyle, he decided to get his own flat and hand in his notice. A brave call! Now he was free to do what he wanted to. It was totally invigorating! A couple of months later he had found a new job he enjoyed and met a girl who ran marathons. He trained with her, which helped him pull further out of the depths and soon he was fit to play again. Approaches from other football clubs followed shortly after.

Mark had the life that many would envy and he lived it to the full. He also decided when it no longer suited him and set out to create a different life that would make more of his sporting talent. He could have carried on, but pulled the rug from under his own feet to drive change. It was the best thing he could have done and set him on the path to success.

Attitude to challenge

There is always challenge in life. The question is whether we are ready and willing. It is also true that we can't take on everything that comes our way, so there has to be a selection process. We choose according to the time of life and what we have space for plus how well the challenge fits with our core talent.

You can access your attitude to challenge at this point in your life by using the challenge grid.

The two vectors in Figure 5.2 determine your approach to challenge:

- Purpose: unless you can see the value in a specific challenge, there is little chance that you will focus on it fully. It has to mean something and you need to see that some benefit will come from taking it on. What matters to you will also change according to your time of life – if you have family, that takes priority; once you have the qualifications you want, your job takes on a greater importance; once you pass sixty, you start thinking about the list of things you want to do before you die.

- Energy: this is the enthusiasm you are willing to put behind a project to make sure it will succeed. You will find your energy increases when the challenge speaks directly to your core talent. Trying to achieve without that is draining and demanding, because you are pushing against your natural flow.

"Energy increases when the challenge speaks directly to your core talent."

Figure 5.2 The challenge grid

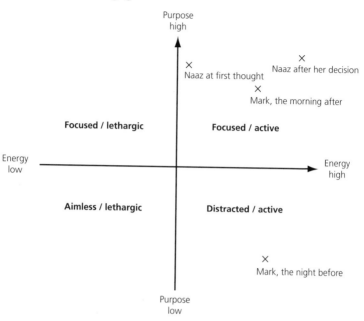

Choosing your challenge

As a serial achiever you will fit into different quadrants according to the challenge. This exercise will help you in two ways:

■ It is a good test of where you are on the life alignment curve. Understanding that will help you identify how you can support yourself in taking the next steps.

■ You can use the grid to review the challenges that face you and work out which is right to persist with. For example. X marks the spot:

   – When Mark was out with his mates at night, he would have been high on energy and low on purpose, leaving him achieving little other than a good time.

   – After his early morning epiphany, his energy levels would have remained high, but now he had purpose. This would have increased his energy levels further as he focused on turning himself round.

- When Naaz received the letter offering the job with the Refugee Council, it was full of purpose for her, but she wasn't sure of her ability, so her enthusiasm and energy weren't as high as they might have been.

- Once she had talked with her boss she felt encouraged and believed in herself more. Then she was able to focus fully and take on the job to great effect.

When you have both energy and purpose, a challenge is really worth taking on.

Let's take a look at the different quadrants.

Distracted / active

This is a very frustrating place. In terms of the life alignment curve, you are probably beginning to feel restless. You know something isn't right, but can't work it out. Part of your restless energy is getting you ready for the next challenge, even though you don't know what it is.

You may attempt to carry on because you can't see the next steps. Or take an impulsive step into the unknown to see what happens. The aim is to look around and see what life has to offer. If this sounds familiar, you are clearly ready to find something that matters to you, so you can use your energy in a productive and satisfying way.

Action:

- Look back at your personal gravity and see what might be holding you back from doing something more satisfying.

- Review your backup and support people to make sure they are on your side. If not, create a bit of distance as you grapple with the next stage of growth.

Aimless / lethargic

This is a tough place to be. You have little sense of purpose –

131

nothing seems to 'light your fire' – so you can see little reason to make an effort. In itself this is debilitating and you will begin to feel down.

As a serial achiever, this may well mean that you are deep in incubation, struggling to find your way out. Remember, this will pass and you will learn a great deal about yourself as you go through it. Getting out to that fabulous time of drive will require you to put in some energy.

Action:

■ Go back to the Fourth Fundamental and revisit the exercises on core talent. If you are feeling very negative, ask for help from someone who knows you well. You may not agree with what they say – listen anyway and 'act as if' the findings are right. Trying it on for size will give you a better sense of what is right.

■ Once you are clear about your core talent, look for something that matters to act on. Again, feel free to ask for help from someone who knows you and cares about you. It may not be right – that's OK. It is the act of looking that starts your energy moving. Take one step at a time and you will amaze yourself.

Focused / lethargic

In this place, you can focus easily on the challenge. Your sense of purpose is high and you want to see the issue dealt with in a positive way. You speak to people about it and wax lyrical about the value of the challenge. On the downside, it doesn't feel like the challenge for you. You don't have much enthusiasm or energy, although you would love to see someone else take it on.

The most likely reason for sitting in this box is that, despite your interest and concern, the task doesn't fit your core talent. It may also be that you are coming to the end of the incubation period, without having yet found the focus for your next step – this is why you don't feel energetic.

Action:

- Use your sense of purpose to support a serial achiever who has the necessary core talent.

- Keep talking to others in the hope of enthusing someone who will want to act.

- Pay attention to your own incubation by noticing the possibilities around you – even if you decide they are not right for you. Putting energy into the search will mean you are more likely to see an opportunity when it arises.

Focused / active

This is the position where purpose and energy meet up – you are in drive on the life alignment curve. To really care about something and to have the energy and ability to act on it is a fantastic feeling and one that most people strive towards.

"Where purpose and energy meet up – you are in drive."

You can reach this place once you know your core talent and understand what matters to you. You will also have a greater self awareness, having gone through an incubation time of personal exploration. As a result, you can now focus on what is important and see results.

Action:

- Enjoy your drive, using your energy to the full. This is a time of great achievement and will feel very satisfying.

- Take good care of yourself – your health and energy levels. Get enough sleep, eat well and have time out with friends periodically. This will support you in doing your best work.

Where are you now?

By now you will understand the needs you have to address if you are to make best use of your core talent:

■ You will have considered that moment where 'fear and dream must collide' and taken a deep breath to think honestly about what you might do next.

■ You have identified those people who provide you with backup and support when you need it. I hope you are also clear on those who, with the best of intentions, tend to hold you back.

■ You will have looked at your approach to challenge and taken first steps in opening up the opportunities available to you.

You are also clear on the five fundamentals of serial achievement – so you have the ground work in place and are ready for action.

So, on to the behaviours of serial achievement . . .

Part 2

Seven behaviours

BEHAVIOUR ONE

Take responsibility

SERIAL ACHIEVERS KNOW THEY DON'T CONTROL LIFE – THEY TAKE RESPONSIBILITY FOR HOW THEY LIVE IT

The moment you take responsibility for your life is also the moment you take off. Life really is what we make of it and it is up to you whether you make it good or bad.

When Su Lissanevitch spent her first winter in Bulgaria she came face to face with mortality. Living alone in temperatures of 15 degrees below zero and thick snow, life came down to the basics of survival. For a time, she found herself focusing on the fact that one day she would die – something we all have to face at some time. Not one to stay negative for long, she decided that if life was so short, then she needed to get on with what she really wanted to do.

One of her values is to concentrate on success, rather than dwell on the risk of failure – not always easy to do. But she has developed a way to handle negative emotions. In her mind, she goes right to the end of the line and works out how she will cope. For example, in renovating her house, she looked at what she could do if there was no money to employ builders. The answer was simple – she would do it herself. Once she knew she could cope and continue to work towards her end goal, then she was able to visualise her lovely new home without problem.

We all have our own ways of coping when times get tough, some of which are unproductive:

- blaming life for bringing bad luck – 'it is just not fair';
- feeling helpless – 'it's not my fault';

■ getting angry and blaming others for the problem – 'How dare you ...'.

The only productive way to get through tough times is to take full responsibility, so you have as much control as possible over the outcome.

What it means to take responsibility

There are many times in life when it is just not possible to influence what has happened or is about to happen, even though the outcome will have a major impact on day-to-day life. So how can it be possible to take responsibility in that situation?

It is a paradox that even when we're not directly responsible for what happens to us, we are totally responsible for how we react. Understanding this is a major step towards being successful.

"We are totally responsible for how we react."

What is responsibility?

The dictionary says it is:

■ having control or authority over;

■ being accountable for our actions.

The reality is that there are many areas of life where we don't have control or authority and where we have to follow a norm or deliver to expectations. As long as the demands are aligned with our values and don't cross the line into what we find unacceptable, most of us are happy to go along with them. Especially when we have some investment in a good outcome, eg: work, friends or family.

However, whatever happens, we are always responsible for our actions and behaviour. For example:

- Being asked to do something doesn't absolve you from responsibility for the outcome. Your response remains in your power – if you choose to go along with the request, you must take responsibility for the outcome.

- When you are challenged by your family or work colleagues, you are responsible for your reaction.

- When you are invited to a prestigious party, it is entirely up to you whether you enjoy yourself and how well you mix with other people.

In short, while you don't control *what happens* to you, you are totally in control of *how you respond to it.*

How does a serial achiever take responsibility?

There are five main areas of responsibility (Figure 6.1):

- Your life and how you choose to use it.
- Your personal reactions.
- Your perceptions of others.
- Your mistakes and failures.
- Your actions and decisions.

My life and choice

The moment you realise that this is your life and it is up to you what you do with it, your attitude changes. This hits people at different times for different reasons:

- It hit Murray Dunlop when he was taking A-levels. The modular course gave him a glimpse of success and he knew he wanted more of it. 'I realised that doing well was directly proportional to hard work – and it was all down to me.' That taste of honey was really helpful!

- Andy Wraith failed her fourth-year dental exams. It was a huge shock, but on reflection, she could see she deserved to fail. Then, ignoring the advice of the dean, who considered it too much to do in one go, she re-sat the exam alongside her finals. Her determination got her through and she managed to pass everything with flying colours!

- Gina Coleman also learned at school that she had control of her own life: 'I realised that no one was to blame but me when I failed. Which also means that it is up to me when I succeed. I can make my own life and seek my own luck.'

Figure 6.1   The five areas of responsibility

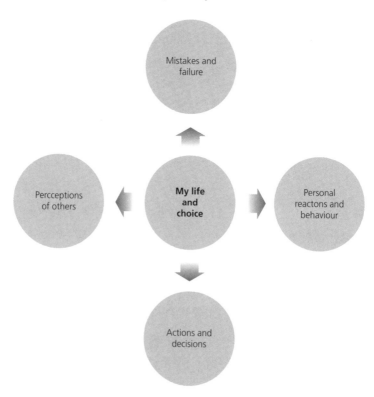

So maybe exams are useful after all! It is both a scary moment and a brilliant one when you know that this is your life and you have the power to determine how it goes. For those ready to take on the challenge, the world becomes their oyster.

EXPLORATION

Think for a moment:

- Are you making the most of your life right now?

- Do you believe you have control over your experience of life? If not, what is stopping you?

- What would life look like if you took full responsibility for your experience?

Someone I respected once said to me: 'You have no right to expect anything from anyone. You are responsible for yourself.' It was a defining moment for me. I came back home and experimented living with that statement. Let me tell you that when I took full responsibility, life was very tiring! I went to the extreme for a couple of days as an experiment and it was eye-opening. I realised just how much I took for granted, how hard I worked to get my own way and how often I blamed someone else if things didn't go well.

Try it yourself some time. Live your life without the expectation than anyone will do anything for you. You will soon discover how you much you rely on the people around you!

The outcome for me was realising that:

- it's fine to get help from others as long as I ask openly and don't make assumptions;

- it does me no good when I just want my own way. I lose respect for myself and the other person;

- once I give up the expectation, I can do far more than I thought I could.

Taking responsibility for your personal reactions

This is the big one: your interpretation of what happens will affect your experience of an event. It is up to you whether you focus on the positive or the negative and whichever you choose will change your experience of life.

"It is up to you whether you focus on the positive or the negative."

When Matthew Taylor failed his A-levels he panicked – for a short time. Then he found a lecturer and asked for help. The end result was that he passed second time and went on to gain a first class degree and an MA. He didn't stop there – the next step was to get elected as a county councillor at the age of twenty-four, campaigning with real intensity for the things he believed in. Matthew is a perfect example of the value of a gutting failure – see what the future looks like without the chance to use your core talent and the mind becomes remarkably focused!

A high percentage of the serial achievers I have met failed or threatened to fail exams and they all quoted this as a major turning point in their lives. Those who chose to take it as a challenge either:

- worked harder, like Andy and Matthew; or
- found another way to succeed in their lives, like Gina.

Either way, they saw the tough time as an opportunity rather than a blocker.

Bill, on the other hand, took success and made it into a dead end. Despite fantastic exam results, he was determined to see himself as a failure. This is a really challenging one – if he sees himself as a failure, yet has good qualifications and a good job – what is he? Failure or success? It has to be failure – because how he sees himself will be how he lives his life.

EXPLORATION

Finish the following questions in three ways. Then make a note of how you feel when you make the statement.

Responsibility	Reaction
I have to:	And that makes me feel:
1.................	1.................
2.................	2.................
3.................	3.................
I choose to:	And that makes me feel:
1.................	1.................
2.................	2.................
3.................	3.................

Notice the difference in feeling when you give responsibility over to another person, 'I have to do it', as opposed to when you take the responsibility on for yourself, 'It is my choice to do it.'

In Gestalt, one of the humanistic psychologies, we talk about 'choosing it the way it is'. In other words, if you can't change what is happening around you, then not only accept it, but actively choose it to be that way. This enables you to take back responsibility for your life and regain some control. It doesn't, however, mean you have to carry on accepting something that isn't right – once you take full responsibility for your response, you are in with a chance of creating some worthwhile change.

As you look at a situation, consider the impact of responding in a negative way and how it will change if you 'choose' the positive. Remember Bill, who managed to make a negative out of a good academic record. You can do anything if you really try!

Perceptions of others

You can't control how other people feel about you, can you? While you can never determine how another person will respond to you – that is their responsibility – your behaviour will certainly have an influence. Therefore, you do have control over what you present to them and the level of attention and awareness you give to their response. So you can:

- think about the impression you want to make on someone before you see them;
- pay attention to how they respond – focus on them as well as yourself;
- have a conversation if you are concerned about their response to what you say or do;
- help them understand the message you want to give;
- take time to listen thoroughly and respond to what has been said, so they feel understood.

Everyone develops their own perceptions, based on personal gravity and direct experience. You can't affect the former, but you can definitely influence the latter. Negative perceptions arise from poor quality contact that leaves friends and colleagues feeling you don't really care about what they think or feel. When the relationship is good, the perception will be good, even if you deeply disagree with each other.

'Acting as if'

Perceptions are particularly important when you stretch your core talent into a new arena or go the next step in your field of expertise. Whenever you begin something new, it is inevitable that you are less confident and not as totally in control as you will be in the future.

You have to take the leap in a way that gives other people confidence, while you build up your strength. We are not talking chutzpah here – where you go ahead even though you know you can't deliver on the promise. This is all about 'acting as if' – you are using your core talent, so you *know* you can do it, even if you *feel* you can't. You also know that you will get better and more sophisticated in the work as time goes by.

'Acting as if' requires that you deliver what people expect or need to see, while refining your ability (Figure 6.2). It works on three levels:

1. Face to the world – you convey confidence to the outside world, both in yourself and your ability to deliver. 'It will be fine and you will do a good job.' You know this is true, because you are committed to doing what it takes.

Figure 6.2 'Acting as if'

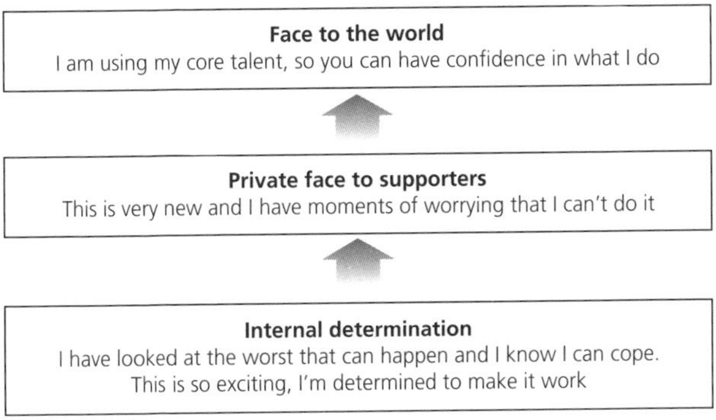

Face to the world
I am using my core talent, so you can have confidence in what I do

Private face to supporters
This is very new and I have moments of worrying that I can't do it

Internal determination
I have looked at the worst that can happen and I know I can cope.
This is so exciting, I'm determined to make it work

2. Private face to your supporters – it is both exciting and a bit scary to move outside your comfort zone with your core talent. Even though you are putting on a confident face to the world, you need to acknowledge your anxiety somewhere. This is where your backup person comes in. Talk through how the new experience went. What went well? How can you improve next time? This way, you will increase your confidence and learn how to refine your work.

3. Internal determination – at a deeper level again, you are confident that you can do it and utterly determined to put in all the effort needed to take this step. You will have looked at the risks, addressing where you need help, as well as clarifying that you will do no harm and can handle whatever comes. The excitement and satisfaction of stretching yourself will help you stay focused on a clear picture of success.

Susan Bull is always conscious of how other people perceive her. 'In retail, people want to associate with success, so I have to manage how they see me and the shop.' So every time she takes a leap into something new, she keeps her face to the world strong and confident, dealing with her 'wobbles' elsewhere.

Of course, taking responsibility requires that you don't 'act as if' in a way that could be damaging of others. This is not the behaviour of a heart surgeon. It is the behaviour of a serial achiever who is breaking new ground for themselves or the world around them and who is taking time to consistently review how they can do the task in a better way.

Managing negative perceptions

When a relationship is not going well it is tempting to assume the other person is in the wrong. It isn't comfortable to consider that your behaviour is doing damage, so of course you look for ways to get off the hook. In fact, whoever is officially responsible, you will always have played your part. And, as ever, you are the only one you can guarantee changing, so managing your own behaviour can be the difference between success and failure.

"Managing your own behaviour can be the difference between success and failure."

EXPLORATION

Choose one person in any area of your life – work, home, social, volunteer, leisure. Think about whether their relationship with you is positive or negative.

If the relationship is positive, consider:

- how you have contributed to it;
- what contribution the other person made to the relationship;
- what you need to do to maintain a positive perception.

If the relationship is negative, consider:

- how you have contributed to it;
- what contribution the other person made to the negativity;
- what you can do to change their perception.

Notice how you feel as you contemplate a negative perception. Do you:

- Rationalise so it is they who have the problem?
- Explain your own behaviour in a way that lets you off the hook?
- Consider how you behaved and what you might have done differently?

When a relationship is struggling under negative perceptions, first decide if the association has had its day, in which case you need to conclude as well as you can and move on.

Second, if you want the relationship to improve, start with yourself:

- Consider how you have contributed to the negative perception. Note the particular behaviour plus what you need to do to create a positive outcome.

- Consider the behaviour of the other person. How does it affect you? How have you responded to date? Then think about how you might respond differently and promote change.

With any of the responses, by taking responsibility you reclaim your own power to create the life you want. You stop letting other people control your view of yourself and your ability. Once you have done this, you have the choice to move forward in the way you want to.

Mistakes and failures

Taking responsibility for mistakes and failure is an important behaviour in serial achievers. Try anything new and you are sure to make mistakes. The benefit is in how you view those mistakes.

- Eversley Felix gives failure little space in his life. A course he set up at work didn't go well and was highly criticised. He just kept on refining until it was top quality and very popular – he was unwilling to give up and accept it as failure. However, he doesn't like mistakes and gives himself a hard time about them. Once he lifts his head up from this, he takes action: 'It's important to be humble, then get on and do something about it.'

- For Peter Fisher, failure was the making of him. After spending some time at his secondary modern school after a failed 11+, he went to see the headmaster and said: 'Look, I want to make something of my life, what shall I do?' He was told to go each lunchtime to the headmaster's study where he would be set extra work. In time, they moved him to the grammar school and he went from strength to strength.

■ Harriet Kelsall thinks that if you dwell on failure, you will fail. Equally, she believes that if you don't think you're going to fail, you won't. 'You just need to be realistic about what it will be like – look at others and see what happens to them. Then be realistic about your ability. I'm not the best, but I'm willing to give it a go and that's what makes the difference.'

So mistakes and failure can give you a real advantage. Unless you are open to this possibility, you'll be obliged to carry on in your safety zone, never testing yourself or learning more about what you can do.

No one likes making mistakes, which is why the experience teaches us so much! I bet you can remember most of the significant mistakes you have made in your life and that you have worked very hard not to make them again! So you become the safest person to take on that task in the future.

Of course, that doesn't mean that this is a pleasant process and your response will probably vary according to whether you tend towards introspection or investigation. With too much introspection, any mistake or failure will be distressing. You will:

■ blame yourself;

■ go over and over what happened and beat yourself up for making the mistake/failing;

■ hold on to the memory for years and bring it out periodically when you are feeling bad about yourself.

However, if you investigate what happened, you will find it easier to take the learning and move on. You will:

■ look back on the situation rationally to understand what happened;

■ do what is necessary to put it right;

■ store up the learning and use it to inform your next action.

A fit of pique

Zena Martin has learned never to make a decision based on spite or pride. When she was twenty-two years old, she worked in a job where she wasn't happy. Rather than sorting it out, she decided to leave on the assumption that she would 'show them'. We all know that one – it's called 'cutting off your nose to spite your face' – and very tempting when we want to be noticed.

In fact, it didn't 'show them' and Zena was left moving on to another job that really was a disaster! She certainly wouldn't do the same thing now and the experience taught her a lot. 'Failure will always teach you something, even if it takes a while for you to get it. Just keep going and it will come to you.'

It is a real advantage to serial achievers – to know that they can try out something new and either it will go well or they will learn something for future reference. The important thing is to forgive yourself, because if you keep beating yourself up, it is much harder to try something new next time.

EXPLORATION

It helps to review mistakes and failure in order to take all the learning you can from a difficult time. However, once you have taken the learning on board, it is vital to give up the self flagellation!

Choose a mistake that you haven't really looked at thoroughly or that haunts you and follow the arrow in Figure 6.3.

Once you are clear what happened and have taken the learning for next time, write down the mistake or failure on a piece of paper. Write it large, colour it in, draw pictures – enjoy yourself as you do it – this is the last time you need to look at it.

Figure 6.3   Learning from mistakes

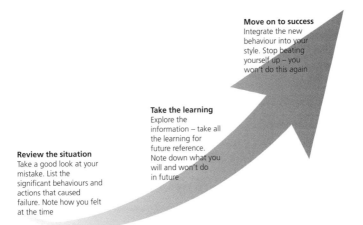

Move on to success
Integrate the new behaviour into your style. Stop beating yourself up – you won't do this again

Take the learning
Explore the information – take all the learning for future reference. Note down what you will and won't do in future

Review the situation
Take a good look at your mistake. List the significant behaviours and actions that caused failure. Note how you felt at the time

As soon as you are ready, tear the paper into little pieces – as small as you can manage, then throw the paper away. This is not one to recycle!

Now you have the learning *and* you have exorcised the memory of the mistake. You can take it out again if you really want to – that is your choice – but you don't need to!

Actions and decisions

Being a serial achiever means taking action and that requires you to take responsibility for the outcome.

Taking responsibility for your choices

Jim Al-Khalili had lectured to local schools on the subject of black holes and the possibility of time travel according to modern physics. The talk was so successful that word got back to the Institute of Physics who run an annual nationwide schools lecture tour. When someone couldn't fulfil their agreement Jim was asked to step in and take his lecture on the road.

People counselled him not to get distracted from his research. He knew there was some sense in what they said, but it was such an exciting opportunity, he chose to ignore them.

In fact he was right to do so. It proved to be the beginning of a public life that has led to a number of television series explaining physics to those who find it hard to decipher, plus books that have been translated into thirteen languages.

There are two lessons in there:

- Follow your heart: if you are keen to follow an opportunity, it is worth a try.
- Whatever you do, take responsibility for your choices.

If it hadn't gone well it would have been down to Jim. And that it went well is down to Jim. The one behaviour that wasn't open to him was to hold someone else responsible for the outcome, whatever it was.

To be a serial achiever, you have to make decisions and no time is more important than when emerging from the incubation period – essentially, you are coming out of the unknown to something new. Whatever you choose to do will carry some level of risk.

The only way to manage the risk is by taking full responsibility. Doing this means you commit to learning what you need to know, thereby increasing your chances of success.

When Craig Fazzini-Jones had the opportunity to move to a job in another company, he was extremely thorough in his exploration of the situation:

- He began by talking to the people he would work with to make sure he was a good cultural fit.
- He talked to people who knew the company by reputation to find out what their experience was.

- He had a long discussion with his wife, Amanda, to get her view on the changes that would result – home/work balance, for example.

- He went through the finances with a fine-toothed comb – this was some serious homework!

- He called up friends that he respected – people who were good at taking rational decisions – and asked them what he had missed.

Because he would be moving from a large company to a smaller one and in a very senior job, he had to be totally sure of his decision. 'I knew there would be nowhere to hide, I couldn't moan to the boss – I would be the boss! This was all down to me.'

He finally decided to do it and because he had been thorough and clear in his deliberations, he was willing to accept the risk. This was his responsibility and there was no turning back.

All serial achievers take on responsibility for their actions. They know you can't serve a probationary period with a life decision, so do all they can to be fully informed.

"You can't serve a probationary period with a life decision."

Only full commitment really engages your energy. Once you are committed, your chances of success increase tenfold. It is amazing how much difference it makes when you are really clear and give your full attention to a task.

On this basis, even if your new venture does eventually fail, you know you gave it your best shot. Think back to the test of a life well used. It is regret, ie, not taking responsibility, that gets us all in the end. When we look back, not trying is the gutting part. Having tried and failed is much more palatable.

EXPLORATION

Look at recent decisions you have made – there are some suggestions in the decision column. Fill in the table below, clarifying the benefits and the risks and being clear whether you are prepared to take full responsibility.

Decision/ action	Benefit	Risks	Willingness to take responsibility
Eg: move to a new job	1 2 3	1 2 3	
Eg: learn to dance			
Eg: have a family			

As you go through the table, notice where you feel sure and where you haven't yet made a full commitment. With the latter, go back over your deliberations to find what is missing. Then do what you need to do to take a fully responsible decision.

Taking responsibility for other people

One of the decisions that comes to many of us is taking responsibility for other people and this can signal real change for a serial achiever. Life stages demand that we care for others as well as ourselves and that affects things we want to do:

- You may start a family and have children to look after.
- Your parents will grow old and need care.
- You might choose a caring profession, such as a teacher, social worker or nurse.

These are times when you need to seek the balance of care, so you look after the other, without losing track of yourself and your own needs in life.

Accepting responsibility

Life has thrown some interesting situations at Jill Black. There has been no time for wallowing in her failures; she has just had to move on to the next challenge. 'As a station commander's wife, I took on the whole RAF family. I was the figurehead, which meant putting on my evening dress and going to the parties. One Christmas, we did seventeen nights out in a row. All I wanted was a boiled egg, yet everyone wanted to feed me – sometimes twice a night!

'And then there was the time when my husband went into the Gulf War. I have never been so low, but I had all the other wives to take care of. Some had never driven further than the shops, so I had to arrange for them to get home. And with the press hounding us, it was all very hard.'

Jill could easily have gone into a panic with this sort of pressure, but it never occurred to her. She just knew she had to get on with it, it was her job, her duty. She had taken responsibility.

Life brings opportunities at every turn – they are just not always what we would expect or choose. Yet, sometimes, the greatest pleasure and reward can come from helping others and seeing them thrive – that's why many people find raising children a delight, if exhausting.

"Life brings opportunities at every turn – they are just not always what we expect."

For serial achievers, the task is to balance other life plans with the new demands. So one reason that Craig Fazzini-Jones was keen on his new job was that it would give him a greater chance of being home before his daughter's bedtime. And Murray Dunlop finds a real delight in becoming an active father. You can work it out, by altering your priorities and deciding what is most important for you at the given time.

A tougher situation is when the caring decision is not of your choosing. Responsibility is much harder then. When Carol (name changed) reached retirement age, her elderly mother was past the point of being able to care for herself. Carol was an active person who enjoyed her leisure activities, sports, her friends and holidays. Now, she was faced with a tough decision. Did she do the caring herself or take the help that was on offer?

When parents or spouses need care, it is hard to turn away. They have been significant for so long and have also done their share of caring for you, so responsibility must certainly be taken. The question is for what? The key is to choose the care that is appropriate on all fronts. Carol had a number of options:

- To take her mother into her own home and care for her there.
- To move back to the family home with her mother so she could stay where she was.
- To employ carers who would provide support.
- For mother to go into a home where they specialised in her condition.
- To call on other family members even though they were less free or able to care.

The situation brings fear, mistakes, failure and duty all to the foreground. Guilt will dictate that Carol do the caring herself. Yet true responsibility means finding the way that serves mother well and allows Carol to live a life well used.

Reflect on a situation that has or will put responsibility for other people on to your shoulders:

- How well did you take the needs of the other person into account – are they comfortable with the arrangements that have been made?
- How well have you looked after yourself in the process? Are you getting the support and respite you need?
- Will you allow yourself to access the support that is available and set out to get it, if not presently available?

The message Carol needed to take in was that her welfare was the most important part of the equation. Unless she looked after herself, she would have little energy to give to her mother. It is really hard to care for another when you are depleted yourself – as Jill will testify. You can do it for a while, but the cost is high.

So true responsibility means looking at a situation from all angles to determine the most appropriate decision for everyone involved. Guilt – while so tempting – must have no place.

And what did Carol do? She did take care of her mother and found all the support she could, so she still had some life of her own.

Luck or responsibility?

When people are successful, it is very tempting to put it all on the shoulders of Lady Luck:

- I've just been lucky.
- They should have had my luck!
- It's all right for some.

Jim Al-Khalili sees himself as having taken the easy options in his life; other people would probably call him lucky. In fact, he has:

- remained positive about the opportunities coming his way, expecting them to come to fruition;

- developed a skill in assessing situations so he can avoid pitfalls;

- taken careful choices, including his gut reaction as well as thinking things through.

So what is luck?

The awful thing about claiming that something is 'lucky' is that it dismisses responsibility. You can't make luck happen, you just have to wait for it to strike unexpectedly. Sometimes that is right and random events do happen to help or hinder our lives for unknown reasons. However, there are other times when what we call 'luck' is much more under our control.

Opportunity of some sort is always around, so you can see luck as our willingness to be open to a given opportunity.

Think about the last time you bought a new car. Suddenly, everyone seems to be driving that very car. In fact, you had the car on your mind, so you were open to seeing it. They have always been there in the same quantity. Our minds are very clever and guide us to what we need to see.

This is the job of mindsets – they channel your mind along a particularly route, so you know where to look:

- If you believe you are lucky, you will see opportunities that help you.

- If you are persistently half empty – you won't be as lucky as your 'half full' neighbour.

- Accepting responsibility means that you recognise that life is not a matter of luck – you have far more control than that.

I've always loved the Eastern saying 'Trust the lord and tie up your camel.' For me, this is what luck is all about. It underlines the varying elements of success: you need to trust that the universe, life or God – whatever you choose to call it – will support you. And you have to show willing and take action. You have to put energy behind the success – after all, no one ever won a race they didn't enter!

"Trust the lord and tie up your camel."

Creating 'luck'

'Luck' is remarkably demanding. To reach the point where other people claim you have been lucky has probably required you to move from one end to another of the life alignment curve, coming out of incubation through a new epiphany. You will have trusted the process:

- followed your restlessness into the unknown;
- made your way through a confusing and possibly difficult incubation period in the belief that it will work out well in the end;
- allowed yourself to take off into a new world of learning and developing.

And you will have tied up your camel:

- reviewed opportunities;
- explored implications;
- asked for help;
- experimented with a new style.

You have to trust your gut instinct and also take action. I'm sure quantum physics can explain why it is that when we show willing and take responsibility for what is going on around us, things begin to go the right way. I don't know why, yet I have seen it happen time and again. Put energy into an idea and you end up with something good. It may not be exactly what you first thought of, more likely it will be even better! Sit back and hope for opportunities and you'll be waiting a long time.

It is summarised nicely in this quote from Goethe:

> *Until one is committed, there is hesitancy, the chance to draw back, always ineffectiveness . . . The moment one definitely commits oneself, then Providence moves, too . . .*

> *Whatever you can do, or dream you can, begin it. Boldness has genius, power and imagination in it.*

Serial achievers take responsibility for what happens and how they respond to it, so life moves with them. Call it luck if you have to, just remember that you create your own luck by accepting the part you have to play!

Where are you now?

You will have a much clearer idea of what it means to take responsibility for your life. While it may feel a bit daunting, you will soon find that it also gives you more freedom and the chance to create the life you want.

You can also review all those good times that you dismissed as 'luck' and see just how hard you worked to make them happen – which again gives you freedom.

So now let's look at building relationships that will support you . . .

BEHAVIOUR TWO

Build relationships

SERIAL ACHIEVERS CARE FOR THE PEOPLE AROUND THEM – THEY KNOW WE ARE IN THIS TOGETHER

Gina Coleman is genuinely interested in people. 'I don't do it for self advancement, it's just the way I am and have always been.' Wherever she worked she liked to introduce herself to people. So from the chief executive to the maintenance person, she knew them all.

The reality is that we are always in relationships one way or another. We can't avoid it. As human beings we function in societies, tribes and families. So the sooner you develop the art of building relationships, the greater chance you have of success.

How relationships build success

It is difficult to over-emphasise the value of relationships to serial achievement. You move through your life, changing to follow your interest and the needs of the time. The path is an interesting one and demands that you keep growing and learning. Some of this you can do on your own, but you will also need people to help you – whether to give you support, provide you with ideas for action or to introduce you to someone who can help.

While a job or pastime may be new to you, it is unlikely to be new in the world – someone, somewhere, will have done a version of it before. Or you will have a friend with a core talent that is close in style, so they can provide support as you adjust to the latest change.

You can have no idea where you will be ten years from now – that's the adventure. To make sure you can access the right people when you need them, you need a strong web of relationships – some of which you already have, some you need to develop. Not only will it bring you joy and excitement, it will be the best investment of time and energy you can make.

What do we mean by relationship?

Relationship is all about making contact with another person. It can happen in all sorts of ways, ranging from a passing smile with a stranger to a full-blown relationship with a life partner or a child.

And, of course, one can lead to another! Helen Hanson met her husband Simon in a crowded early morning commuter carriage, just through a smile! And this is a feature of every relationship – you never know where the smallest contact will take you, because:

- they are organic and keep developing;
- they grow from small beginnings;
- you can influence how they progress.

Whether through chance meetings or organised network events, serial achievers understand that relationships provide some of the best learning there is. In fact, they may be the difference between success and failure of your next life chapter. Looked at in that way, it is well worth understanding how to make the most of the relationships you have.

The importance of trust

The factor that underpins everything good in a relationship is trust. With trust, you can achieve a great deal and overcome problems when they arise. If there is no trust, then problems become breaking points from which there may be no recovery.

When we trust another person, we assume:

- they have our best interests at heart;
- we can believe what they say;
- they do what they have said they will do.

In fact, what we know them for today will be what we know them for tomorrow – they are consistent and positive.

"The first step is to be trustworthy yourself."

The first step is to be trustworthy yourself. Trust takes a long time to build up, yet is lost in seconds – and recovering it is a long job. So make this the cornerstone of any relationship you have. Remember, you won't know at the outset which one is going to be important, so start as you mean to go on with all relationships.

Losing trust

Lack of trust in a workplace can drastically change how people feel about their employers. Barbara Evans worked for a travel company and really enjoyed her time in the job. Pay wasn't great, but she got lots of opportunity to travel and met some great people.

The leadership had always claimed they were open and honest, so when forced to make redundancies, it was assumed they would do it in the best way possible. They were clear that everyone would be treated the same and employees trusted their word.

When Barbara was moved to a role in human resources, she discovered that all was not as it seemed. When it came to paying a bonus, based on percentage of salary, managers were getting a much higher percentage than staff.

It wasn't the variation that mattered – Barbara was prepared to see that there was a differential in value to the company. It was the fact that they said one thing and did another. As a result, even though she wasn't on the redundancy list, she left for another job.

It is the same in every relationship. Claim one thing and do another and you will lose the confidence of the other person. You then either have to work very hard to heal the trust or give up and go your separate ways. Because the implications are so severe, better to err on the side of being trustworthy at all times.

Relationship as teacher

Degrees and training courses will give you skills. It takes relationships to help you understand people and yourself.

On a personal level

Think back to personal gravity (Second Fundamental). Your own gravitational pull contains much of your learning about life and people. It is so easy to hold on to those early truths, without re-evaluating whether they still serve you. If you want a quick evaluation, try getting into an honest relationship – that will give you all the information you need!

People close to you – a partner, adolescent or adult child – will make it very clear what they think of your assumptions. Data is all around you – your job is to listen fully, then act on what you learn.

You can maximise learning by:

- recognising that you make a contribution to every situation, good and bad, and that your own behaviour is the one thing you can control;

- noticing when people respond well to you and how you were behaving at the time – so you can do the same again;

- looking back on difficult times to review how you contributed and what you might have done differently;

- asking people you trust for feedback on the impact you make – they will be full of helpful information;

- when you find yourself blaming another person, check first on your own contribution to the difficulty.

In a work situation

Work colleagues and acquaintances will have similar information to your close family and friends, but are less likely to tell you. If you work in big organisations there may be learning opportunities that give you direct feedback, such as 360 degree feedback, and annual appraisals. They can be tough, but extremely useful when done well – so make sure you give them quality time.

If you work in your own small business, your main relationships may be with customers. In which case, you may only know there is a problem when work is cancelled. Keep asking for feedback and focus on building trust, so people will speak out when dissatisfied. Even if you still lose that particular piece of work, you have information so you can change your approach next time.

Dave Pack has a life motto from his early years. 'The best people are the most genuine.' It still works today. Working in the music business has added some important lessons about relationships that work everywhere:

- Get on with people: it will take you furthest, on and off the bandstand.

- Always be willing to help out. Taking on last minute gigs to cover sickness has given Dave the chance to show what he can do, to great advantage.

- Never expect the phone to ring. You have to get out there and make it happen – and you will do that through the relationships you build.

Dave has only ever auditioned once in his career – for his first cruise ship. Since then he has focused on doing a good job – 'I can't afford a bad day – the word gets around' – and building links to the significant people. A naturally quiet person, it is not that easy for him to do, yet he keeps going and takes up every opportunity that will put him in front of the right people. As a result, he now works regularly in London's West End.

How to build good relationships

Barbara Evans uses her relationship skills all the time in policing. 'I just like meeting people and I'm not afraid of sitting down to listen and interact with them.' It serves her well in her job 'on the beat' as a member of the Community Action Team, enabling her to gather relevant intelligence when needed.

The key words here are 'like' and 'listen'. The more interested you are in someone, the more chance of getting on to their wavelength. And by listening, you find out what sort of relationship you want or need to build with this person.

Good relationship revolves around common interest, good intention and trust. Achieving this requires you to:

- listen well;
- show empathy;

- be appropriately honest;
- show interest and support;
- resist jumping to conclusions.

Listen well

This is the magic one. It is remarkable how few people really listen! If you can crack this one you gain a head start in any relationship.

"It is remarkable how few people really listen!"

Listening? I don't think so!

Picture the scenario: you are in the supermarket doing your shopping when you meet a friend you haven't seen for a while. You discover they have just come back from holiday, so you suggest pausing in the coffee shop for a while so you can hear all about it.

As you sit over coffee, your friend begins to talk about their time away. The story sparks interesting memories in your mind, so you wait for a pause to tell your own story. Soon you are the focus of attention.

The outcome is that:

- you know a little about your friend's holiday;
- they know a lot about your last two holidays;
- you have missed the fact that your friend sounds low – maybe it wasn't such a good holiday after all!

You walk away from the interlude feeling fine. You had a good chat and enjoyed tripping down memory lane. Your friend on the other hand is probably wondering what that was all about. You offered coffee so you could hear about their holiday and they ended up listening to you.

If that sounds familiar, keep reading. There are some simple things you can do to improve your listening skill:

- Focus your attention on the other person – to do this, put your own thoughts and concerns on the back-burner. The truth is that everyone has something interesting about them and your job is to find it.

- As soon as you don't understand something, ask an open question to find out more. An open question requires more than 'yes' or 'no' as an answer, eg: Tell me more about it; What else did you do; How did you respond?

- When you think you understand, check your assumptions – remember you will be filtering everything you hear through your personal gravity, so may misunderstand. Do this by summarising – 'so you are saying …'.

- Don't forget to look at them – it shows that you are listening, encourages them to continue speaking and you will learn a lot from facial expressions.

- Give encouragement through nodding sometimes and making small comments: 'really', 'wow', 'I see'. Just watch that you don't do this too much or you may sound impatient!

These behaviours will feel rather false at first – new behaviour always does. But you will get used to it and it will be add significant depth to your conversations.

One other trick is notice the behaviour of people who listen well to you. You can then try it on for size and see if it suits you. You will soon find your own style.

Show empathy

Empathy is a natural state for some people – remember Jim Al-Khalili who can make physics easy by understanding what other people need. Essentially, when you show empathy, you put yourself in the shoes of another person and see the world from their perspective. If you have had a similar experience yourself, this is relatively easy:

- Remind yourself what the experience was like.
- Think about the other person and consider how they are different from you.
- Taking those differences into account, how do you suppose they might feel about the situation?

If you haven't had a similar situation, then you need to engage your imagination:

- Imagine you are in the specific situation, what might you feel or do?
- What would be easy or difficult for you? What help or support might you need?
- Apply that thinking to the person concerned and consider how you might offer the support or help they need.

The important thing to remember about empathy is that no one gets it right all the time. It is fine to get it wrong as long as you don't insist on your view. Instead of making assumptions, say: 'If that was me, I think I'd feel … Is it like that for you?' They can then agree or tell you the way it actually is.

"It is fine to get it wrong as long as you don't insist on your view."

If you are not used to thinking in this way, then have a practice. Choose people you know well and try looking at life through their eyes. Then ask if you got it right.

If you are someone who really can't empathise, there are ways to manage this:

- Assume you will be missing something and make a point of

asking 'How do you feel?', or 'How can I help?' It may not feel necessary to you, but it will help the other person and give you any information that you will have jumped over.

- Let those close to you know that you don't respond to subtle messages. Once they understand this, they will know not to wait for you to ask and just say what they want you to hear.

- Surround yourself with people who are good at empathy, so you can work as a team.

Be appropriately honest

Setting out to be honest is a necessity for serial achievers, because it is the basis of trust. Whether you need to explain yourself or have something you want to tell another, erring on the side of honesty will bring benefits in the long run. In every relationship, implicit or explicit agreements are made about the most appropriate way to do this.

Formal relationships

In these situations, contracts and agreements should have been worked out formally so everyone is clear about what is expected. This is particularly important if you are in business with other people, but the same rules apply where you are part of a team working for an employer. In every work situation you need high levels of openness and honesty to ensure that you run the business well together. Things can fall down if no one is willing to tell the truth. So, if you don't have agreements in place:

- Sit down with your colleagues and agree how you want to work together. Make sure this includes honest feedback and discussion – it will be a saviour in tough times.

- Adopt the agreed ways of behaving yourself and always be honest about your mistakes, problems and concerns. This will encourage others to talk to you when they have concerns.

■ If you hear gossip, take action to stop it. This will help the specific situation and increase trust.

Informal relationships

Building a strong network means you meet all sorts of people. Some you will get to know well and others will never move beyond acquaintance. In each situation you need to decide the appropriate level of honesty.

Use the following prompts as a guide:

■ What will be the effect of not telling the truth about yourself or others? If staying silent will be negative, look for ways of opening the conversation. If it won't make any difference, let it go.

■ What will be the impact if the other person discovers you have been silent – what will it do to your relationship?

■ If you were in the other position, what would you want?

If you decide that it is right to tell the truth, start by practising empathy. If it were you, how would you like to be told?

You can then work out a plan of action. If you are the problem, then do your own talking. If it's about another, consider what will enable them to take the comments seriously, eg, make sure they hear from someone they trust. Whatever happens, always be ready to listen to what the other person has to say, whether you agree with it or not.

Show interest and support

The fact that someone showed an interest was the starting point of a new life for Lucy Shuker. Leaving hospital after her accident, she met Peter Norfolk who has won numerous competitions and medals for his wheelchair tennis. While chatting to her in the car park, Pete and his friend, Andy Mac, lifted her from her day chair and put her into a tennis wheelchair. She could tell immediately how much easier it would make moving around the court.

Without Peter taking an interest, she might never have found her way into competitive tennis. With his help she began to train, have coaching and entered into her first British tournament. Now she is the top women's player in the UK.

"A small action can be the turning point."

Your interest could make an equivalent difference to someone you know. It doesn't need to be life-saving – an interested conversation can start new ideas forming or a small action can be the turning point.

Keep in mind the incubation stage of the life alignment curve – it only takes something small to spark the next move. You may not even notice the comment or think the conversation is of little value, yet it may be just what the other person need to hear.

So pay attention and be interested in others and you could make a major difference. And sometimes taking the focus off yourself changes your own perspective and can be a turning point for you too – it's a win, all round!

Resist jumping to conclusions

This is the easiest thing to do in a relationship. You think you understand and, fuelled by your own personal gravity, you jump to a conclusion.

Eversley Felix did just this when asked to go and see his boss. She was a naturally quiet person and didn't normally say much, so Eversley had no idea what the meeting was about. After a sleepless night worrying that he was in for a very tough conversation, he sat down in her office. 'You are doing a really good job and I'm concerned that I might lose you. So would you mind if I give you a pay rise?'

How easy it is to assume the worst! We all do it and we can make heavy weather for ourselves. The moment you assume you understand is the time to pause for breath:

- What were the signs that led you to make the assumption?
- Check against your personal gravity – is your assumption a familiar one?
- Consider the different ways you might interpret the signs.
- Check out your assumptions with the person concerned or someone else who knows you well.

It may be that your personal gravity has taught you to spot the signs of particular behaviour so you are generally accurate. It is also possible that you are jumping to conclusions without taking into account the gravity and norms of the other person.

EXPLORATION

Make a list of the most significant people in your present network – long-standing contacts that you value and new people you want to get to know better.

Consider them against the key elements of a good relationship to see how well you are doing and where you need to focus your attention. Give yourself a score out of 10 for each one (10 = great at it; 1 = not great at all!). If you come in below 40, then it is time to review the relationship and see what you can do to improve or change it.

	Name:	Name:	Name:	Name:
I listen thoroughly to what they have to say				
I take time to understand their situation and empathise				
I speak honestly about problems – mine and theirs				
I am interested in them – their lives and interests				
I think carefully before I jump to a conclusion about them or a situation				
Total score out of 50				

Notice the difference between each person:

- When you are doing well, which of these behaviours might you use with someone else?
- If you are doing badly, consider how important the relationship is to you. If not, it may be time to let it go.

If you are committed, then make out a plan for how you might improve the present level of trust and connection.

Every relationship will teach you something

Because people are so very different, relationships won't always be easy. However, the tough times are often where you learn most about yourself and other people.

Derek Ffoulkes learned a great deal about his personal strength when working his way through a difficult situation with his colleagues. In one of his early roles he was involved in a disciplinary action as a witness, including giving evidence. Feelings were running high, including questions of loyalty. It ended with Derek being 'sent to Coventry' for several months by the team he managed.

It was an extremely demanding time for him. 'It was a case of me or my team and I was determined it wasn't going to be me who lost out as a result of doing the right thing. It really helped to build my resilience. It also taught me that, however good a relationship you have with people, there will always be other influences.'

This is worth bearing in mind. However much effort you put in, it may all come unstuck for a reason beyond your control. At times like this it is important to remember the two key messages from Behaviour One: first, the need to be honest in reflecting on your role in the situation; and second, that while you may not be in control of what happens to you, you are in control of how you react to it.

The experience helped Derek crystallise his thoughts:

- However difficult things are, you can use your mental strength to deal with it – and facing a tough time like this one will teach you just how strong you are.
- Nothing stays the same forever and the learning will help you deal differently with tough times in the future.

Derek continued to do his job, keeping conversations to those about specific areas of the work, until ultimately his colleagues came round. 'The Christmas lunch was coming up and I decided I wasn't going. Then one or two of the team said: "Look, we would like you to be there, come along and join us." So I did.'

He took learning from this experience into his next roles in business, knowing that even when the going gets really tough, he can survive.

The value of a network

Imagine you are just coming out of a long and rather confusing incubation period. Your energy is high, because at last you have a sense of direction – it might just have been something you read, but it brought all your thoughts into line and you can see exactly what you need to do. How exciting!

This is exactly what happened to Miriam McLoughlin. Her epiphany came when sitting in a master class. She realised the stage wasn't for her, but supporting others, through being an actors' agent, might well be. It was a relief to have some sense of direction and she was buzzing with energy.

The question then was 'which way to turn?' Because she had good relationships with her teachers, she could go direct to them and ask for advice on the next steps. They then accessed their networks to put her in touch with people doing the job she thought she wanted, so she could get a realistic viewpoint. And from there she was able to reach a range of people who might be able to help her.

Miriam could have gone to books, magazines, websites – all would have given her a view on the life of an actor's agent. The network approach gave her something different and very special – the chance to have a conversation with someone who knew the ins and outs of the job. Not to mention the fact that a number of people now knew an enthusiastic young woman who was looking for a job.

How to network

Every serial achiever has a network of people who help them to use their core talent. Some do this consciously, looking out for people whose company they enjoy and who they want to get to know. Like Helen Hanson, who loves chatting to new people and introducing one to another across different networks – a habit that led to a job offer just as she was thinking of returning to work after having children.

Others allow it to happen organically, trusting interested people will notice what they do and pass the word around. Jim Al-Khalili is a great example of a serial achiever who lets his natural sociability work for him. Through his success in giving lectures to school kids on the Big Bang, someone else spoke to TV programmers about him and they then approached him about making a series called *Atom*.

The main ways of getting to know other people are:

- take every opportunity to meet people;
- be generous with your core talent;
- link other people together;
- be a joiner;
- go to gatherings.

Take any opportunity

There are endless opportunities to get talking to people if you are willing, yet it is easy to feel shy or foolish. Friends will invite you to interesting events with their other friends, work will hold parties for the whole business and holidays will provide a complete new set of people.

The trick is to chat just for the delight and because the other person is interesting. You have no idea where a mutual benefit may arise – whether that is a new friendship, a soul mate or a business opportunity. Don't worry about that – just be yourself and enjoy. The rest will take care of itself – just like it did for Jim.

"Chat just for the delight … be yourself and enjoy."

Be generous with your core talent

As human beings we give what we receive – if someone is generous to you, you are more likely to be generous in return. So if you want to build a relationship, role model the style of contact you are looking for.

You have a core talent that you enjoy and that you can use relatively easily, so be liberal with it. Offer your help to people, with or without payment, if you can. Not only will you demonstrate how good you are, people will remember and tell others about you.

If you like the sound of this, remember two things:

1. Don't wait for others to give to you first – you might never take any action! Being generous in this way is not an everyday norm, so take the opportunity to differentiate yourself.

2. Don't expect anything in return – do it for the delight of giving and helping someone. If you focus on the response, it will affect the recipient and you set yourself up for disappointment. Life itself will 'pay back' but probably from an entirely different place. So just get on and enjoy the process for its own sake.

An act of generosity

I was on the receiving end of such an act of kindness many years ago and I still remember it. My husband wrote to Paul Gayler, the executive chef at the Lanesborough Hotel, because I was so impressed with his style of vegetarian cooking. The request was for Paul to come and say 'hello' when John took me for dinner on my birthday. In fact, Paul entered into the spirit of it and gave us both a wonderful evening to remember. Not only that, he invited me to cook in the kitchens whenever I wanted to. So for about three years, when I needed a break, I would go and cook for a day. I met some lovely people and learned a lot about food, presentation – and how hard people work in hotel kitchens!

There was nothing for Paul to gain, other than witnessing our total delight. Yet I have waxed lyrical to many people over the years about his generosity, including to a friend who ran events. My story remained in her mind, so when looking for somewhere to hold a prestigious dinner for journalists and government ministers – she went to the Lanesborough.

Paul and I are still in touch periodically and I look forward to the day when I can do something for him in return. So the message is – do something that will give you pleasure and help others. Do it for the delight and be open to what might come as a result.

Link people together

Zena Martin is brilliant at this. She is a natural networker and delights in bringing people together. My first coffee with her was a real experience. As we talked about life, her mind was buzzing with people she might introduce me to and who might be able to help me. And by the time I logged on the next morning, I had two introductory emails.

There is a theory called the 'six degrees of separation' that states we are all only six contacts away from anyone! More than just a fun party game, this is something really useful to aim for. As long as you are willing to share your contacts with other people, you open up the possibilities significantly.

There are a few simple rules to remember:

- Take real care of the people in your network. Make sure you behave respectfully, so they don't feel over-exposed.
- If you are in any doubt that your contact won't want to know a new person, get in touch first and find out.
- Never gossip or give information that has been told to you in confidence. If in doubt – keep your mouth shut!

- Be willing to talk about yourself – what you are good at, your aspirations, what makes you who you are, what excites you and what you hate. This way they will know when it would be helpful to link you to someone else.

- Listen carefully to what your contact says about themselves and ask them questions to make sure you have understood. That way you have the best chance of being able to help.

Be a joiner

There are many organisations that are designed to bring together people with a common interest. They set out to build networks, so give you a hand in reaching out.

As a serial achiever, you will understand the importance of time with like-minded people who can stimulate your thinking and provide support or ideas you haven't thought of yourself. For example:

- Charitable groups where you can meet others who are passionate about a similar cause to yourself.

- Football clubs: stay fit or support your favourite club.

- Business clubs provide the opportunity to meet people who are keen to share business learning and mutual benefit.

- School committees: help out at your kids' school and meet like-minded parents.

The list goes on. All you have to do is explore. Surf the web, talk to people you know, read books and magazines, then follow the option that catches your attention.

As Helen contemplated returning to work after having three children, she felt a little daunted. Could she still do it or would she have lost the knack? Before motherhood, she had headed up learning and development for a large insurance company, so knew she was good at her job. It was just the six-year gap taking its toll.

Since her eldest went to school, Helen had always helped out when needed. One day, after telling the 'parent read' class story, the teacher congratulated her on doing it so well: 'You must have done this before, the way you involved all the children in talking about the story line.' Of course, she was right – replace senior executives with kids and you have the same core talent shining through. Just that one comment reminded her how much she enjoyed her work and showed that she still had it in her.

Go to gatherings

Put yourself around people who have similar interests and are also keen to make contact. You can chose any occasion that brings people together – as long as you are interested and will have the chance to chat.

Of course, in any gathering you have the chance to talk, as long as you make the best of it. Zena, for all her amazing networking skills, is really quite shy. Because she understands the value of the process, she forces herself to get out there to say 'Hello'. It is never easy; just remember that if you feel that way, so will other people in the room. So stepping out to speak to someone may be a real gift to them, saving them from having to do it themselves!

- Tell the person your name and expect them to forget it!

- Develop an easy entrance phrase to get you started: Have you travelled a long way? What did you think of the last speaker? What is your interest in this meeting?

- Give a bit of information about yourself early on in the conversation, so they don't feel hi-jacked by some unknown.

- Be really interested – and if you can't find something to be interested in, move on.

- Get used to disengaging yourself from a conversation – see someone you know and want to talk to; say 'good to meet you – enjoy the rest of the event' then leave; excuse yourself to visit the loo – whatever feels easiest.

Hold your interest throughout and be wholehearted. If you are genuine, people will know that and want to spend more time with you.

"If you are genuine, people will want to spend time with you."

EXPLORATION

Think about your present network – who are they and where did they come from? Choose one person you know well and consider the following questions to find out how well you know them. If you know the answer, give yourself the allotted score. If not, then give yourself zero:

Question	Answer	Score
Where do they live?		3
How do they spend their time – work, volunteer work, caring, hobbies?		5
Name the three people closest to them (score 2 per person)		6
Name the activity they enjoy most – hobbies, pastimes and relationships		6
Name one interest you have in common		5
Name three opportunities for you to help them (score 2 per opportunity)		6
Name three things that make them special (score 3 for each)		9
Total		40

If you score less than 35 you are not be making the most of the relationship.

As you review your answers, pay particular attention to the question about what you have in common. If you find there is little to put in this box, then it may well be time to get out and meet more people.

As a serial achiever, you will grow and blossom, needing different people. This doesn't mean that you cast others aside – if the interest is still there, carry on the relationship. If you are just acting out of duty, then decide if that is the right thing to do and take it from there.

Where are you now?

Looking at the relationships you have built to date and understanding what you need to do to improve them is a really useful exercise:

- You have a better understanding of what it takes to build a good relationship, so you can take action both with existing people and new contacts.
- You understand the importance of your network and can take action accordingly.
- You can consider the significant people you know and define where there are gaps in your knowledge of them.

I hope you have also got a sense of how fascinating a good network is – people are just so interesting, once you make the effort to know them. You will also see just how interesting you become to others when you put effort into your existing relationships.

With the stability a good network can give you, let's go on to consider how you can embrace change ...

BEHAVIOUR THREE

Embrace change

SERIAL ACHIEVERS ENGAGE WITH CHANGE – THEY KNOW THAT'S WHERE OPPORTUNITY LIES

Andy Wraith knew it was time for a change, she just had no idea what it was. She had made lists until blue in the face, but got no nearer to a solution. Tidying up her desk one day, she picked up a copy of the *British Medical Journal* and fell half-heartedly on the special appointments section. 'Tribal Women. Do you want a life changing experience? BBC 2 is looking for women with a sense of adventure to spend a month living with a tribe in a remote area of the world.'

Her imagination fired, Andy responded and was invited for an interview on camera. 'I was very excited, the idea of living in such a different situation was really appealing. I felt this was what I had been waiting for; the turning point that would help me find a new and exciting direction.' She clearly came across well and so was accepted as one of the tribal wives.

As part of the Mentawai tribe, she lived in a family with four women, two young boys and two little girls. She had an interpreter for part of the time, otherwise had to manage with sign language. The experience helped her to clarify a number of questions in her life:

- Freedom and creativity are really important to her.
- She wants to help make the world a better place.
- She is definitely not made for communal living – she is happy on her own and her fulfilment is not going to come through family life.

She saw women who were restricted just by the tough way of life and it made her grateful she was born in the UK. And very determined to make the most of the life she had – because she could.

Embracing change

As a serial achiever you need to do more than accept change, you need to embrace it. This requires you to:

- welcome each new challenge for the way it will stretch you;
- use it to refine and build your core talent;
- accept rough times as an opportunity to review your personal gravity so you can make the necessary re-alignment.

Change is the engine for serial achievers. It tempts you into the next life chapter and accompanies you on the life alignment curve. As you adjust your personal gravity, so you become increasingly able to manage complex situations. All of which gives you the advantage in a fast-moving world, adding value to your working environment and to the people around you.

Embracing change gives you the edge and ensures there is always something new, interesting and exciting around the corner. Life won't be simple and easy, but it will certainly keep you engaged and enthusiastic, whatever your age or stage.

"Embracing change gives you the edge."

Where does change come from?

Change comes at us from all directions:

- from the world around us – climate change, economic change, social change;

- the world of work – new jobs, redundancy, setting up your own business;
- close personal life – loss of close family, falling in love, having children.

Your job as a serial achiever is to look out for the changes that will benefit you and that you can use to advance your learning or your occupation.

World/community change

If we are to manage global change, serial achievers will be the ones to do it, on both the large and small scale – so don't sit back, thinking this bit is not to do with you. You may have just the core talent that is needed to manage a tough situation in your neighbourhood, town or business. You may be just the MP your area needs or just the person for an assignment overseas – nothing is impossible.

The key is to choose the cause or concern that really matters to you and then see how you can best respond.

Letting your values drive you

Simon Duffy has always had a strong desire to help people lead full and happy lives. He also has an abiding value that demands he keeps a positive attitude towards the type of world he wants to live in and his core talent of conceptualising graphically means he can see what transformed systems need to look like.

For as long as he can recall, his vision has been for a 'welfare system that doesn't screw people up'. To play his part in making this happen, he has had to embrace change at all levels:

- Challenging the Civil Service to find ways of improving the system – not easy to do in such a well established organisation.

■ Living with complexity and uncertainty as he came up with strategies that might tempt local government into change.

■ Managing his own frustration because everything takes longer than he wants it to – and doing his best not to be too 'prickly'!

The success he is most proud of is Inclusion Glasgow – a small organisation that provides supported living for people who have been in long-term institutional care. He set it up on his own in 1996 as a small organisation that would maintain its values and build real relationships. Since then it has gone from strength to strength, supporting other small organisations to join in the task.

The demands of his path are certainly not easy, yet his determination to create change has kept him focused on action. And his values mean that 'most big decisions feel inevitable. I just have to consider whether I can live with myself, then the next step becomes obvious.'

Like Simon, you have to think about what matters to you and choose the battles you are prepared to fight:

■ Use your values as a measure of what you need to do to feel good about yourself.

■ Take responsibility for your responses to what you hear. If you feel moved, consider what you might do to help.

■ Recognise that you can make a difference, however small. And may be an action you take could be one that creates a groundswell of action from others like you – you will never know unless you try.

Remember the test of a life well used (see Introduction) and make sure you do something useful with your good ideas. Don't look back when ninety years old and regret you didn't try to make a difference.

The world of work

The world of work provides serial achievers with fantastic opportunities for change – there is a new life chapter at every turn! Challenge is constant and talent is always in demand. Not to mention the fact that work becomes a nightmare if you can't embrace change wholeheartedly.

"Talent is always in demand."

If you are employed by an organisation, you will be required to keep beating the competition or improving the service. This may mean extra work and late nights, but will also give plenty of scope for new ideas, new roles and interesting work.

If you have chosen to set up your own business, then you have created endless opportunity for change and review. You also know that the key to success is staying ahead of the curve, so your desire to embrace change will be pivotal to your success.

However you spend your working day, you will be facing:

- ■ increasing demands on your time and energy;
- ■ review and challenge leading to change in targets, workload and outputs;
- ■ requests for innovation to keep ahead of competitors.

You will also have discovered that most important of facts – that people who are able to manage change – even invite it – will be the ones who are sought after. It makes sense – if life and work are about constant change, then people who respond well will deliver the best results.

EXPLORATION

Think back over your working week – whether that be running your own business, running a home or going out to a job. Look at the changes you faced, whether forced on you, chosen by you or avoided. Consider how well you used the change – did you make the most of it or could you have done something differently?

	Action taken	What might you have done differently?	What will you do now?
Changes forced upon you			
Changes you instigated			
Changes you avoided			
Change opportunities you haven't yet picked up			

As you reflect, notice how you respond to the changes:

■ Embracing change. Do you enjoy opportunities as they arise? If so, pay attention to how easily you let yourself go with the delight and excitement. Reflect back on the 'lift' elements of your personal gravity and see how you might make even better use of them in your work.

■ Deflecting change. Do you moan and groan about the demands placed on you? If so, notice what you are afraid of and how you might be more positive. Refer back to your personal gravity and consider what might be holding you back.

The better you get at embracing and welcoming change, the more fun life will be and the more opportunity will come to your door.

Close personal life

If you truly embrace change then you need look no further than relationships to keep you supplied with interesting challenge and opportunity. They will teach you most about yourself and other people and by taking on changes as they arise, you have a much better chance of success.

Serial achievers manage relationships well. This doesn't mean it will be easy or straightforward – no relationship ever is – but by grasping the need for change, they remain aware. Their biggest asset is the ability to hold quality conversation that states the problem and opens up a discussion about how to deal with it positively. This willingness to explore and adapt keeps the relationship flexible and interesting.

If you don't think you're good at this, refer back to Behaviour Two and the section on listening.

Children present a delightful and sometimes vexing challenge. By their nature they change every day and expect their parents and grandparents to stay up to speed. I recall the day a colleague told us: 'When I went to bed last night I had a lovely amenable son, when I woke this morning he had changed into "Kevin"!' Sound familiar?

By entering into any relationship you take on an implicit contract to keep changing, because:

- new life is born;
- partners and friends choose new projects and hobbies that occupy them;
- they want to move house, country or job;
- people reach the end of their lives and die;
- friends marry and you move a step down in the hierarchy.

The list is endless.

Shutting your eyes and ears, assuming it will all go away, doesn't work. The whole relationship becomes rigid and any change is a major disturbance that takes you by surprise. If you pay attention to people, holding regular and open conversation, then you are more likely to adapt at the required pace.

Remember, this is a particularly important area for serial achievers. One of your basic needs is for backup and support and these strong alliances need high degrees of flexibility to remain effective and positive.

EXPLORATION

Choose an important relationship in your life to explore. Look at the table below and underline the descriptions that best describe the relationship:

Inflexible relationship	Flexible relationship
Not interested in conversation	Talk regularly together
Little interest in spending time together – preoccupied when together	Enjoy each other's company
Take relationship for granted – don't understand what matters	Understand what they want from the relationship and put in the effort to give and receive
Unaware of the other person and their needs	Conscious of what the other person might need and ready to change accordingly
Focus on self – little support for the other	Provide backup/support for work/achievement

Note where you have greatest underlining – what does this tell you about the flexibility of this relationship?

■ Inflexible relationships are light on adaptability and attention because each person is primarily self-focused, so unaware of any changes the other person might need. It may feel OK right now, but you will soon start to feel isolated and alone. If you have underlined any of these statements, look at what you would need to do to make the relationship more flexible.

▪ Flexible relationships include plenty of positives, providing strong backup and support. Both people work at keeping the connection alive, changing according to the needs of the other person. If you have underlined any of these statements, then continue what you are doing – it is working well!

Staying aware of the other person's needs will require you to flex and adapt your usual behaviour. It may feel challenging, but it will certainly be worth it, both for your own learning and for the sake of the support you can give each other.

Is change always right?

When you don't agree with the reasons for a change or have a problem with how it is being implemented, then careful thought is needed. Sometimes it is possible to influence things for the better, in which case it is worth hanging in there.

However, there are also occasions when your personal values are challenged and you are powerless to act. In that case, the change you may need to embrace is that of walking away.

Decisions of this sort become much easier once you know where your boundary lies. Revisit the Fourth Fundamental to define what your values are and use them as a benchmark to help you decide the best course of action:

▪ like the junior leader whose boss tried to use him as a 'fall guy' rather than face the music from employees himself;

▪ and the employee whose new leader had talked a good game at interview, then set about behaving in a way that was totally at odds, all the time blaming the employee for the problems;

■ or the person who had to choose between being embarrassed in public by their friend's outrageous behaviour or call a halt.

For all these people, the only real answer was to walk away. If you have tried to do the right thing and nothing works, then sometimes you will need to do the same and move on.

The value of change

Change takes three main forms and whatever the form, there will be a huge amount to learn about yourself:

■ Traumatic change.

■ Changes that come to us.

■ Changes we choose to take on.

Changes vary in impact from extremely exciting to devastating. The more control you have, the less challenge to your personal gravity, so the greater the delight in the early stages. Of course, every change will provide some form of challenge to the status quo – that is why they are so useful as learning opportunities.

Traumatic change

This will always be extreme and provide the toughest challenge. Consider the loss of a parent – something we will all go through. In addition to the sheer grief, all your assumptions about what it means to be the child rise to the surface. Logically, you know you are an adult, but there has always been someone there to act as a buffer. Now you are face to face with your own mortality. You have to truly see yourself as the 'grown up' who is next in line. This is a big challenge to personal gravity and can weigh you down for quite a long time.

Avoiding the feelings will push them into the background, but only until the next tough event causes them to rise up again. So take the time to reflect on what they tell you about yourself.

This could be just the moment to change worn out mindsets that have been holding you back.

Changes that come to us

Even though they may be someone else's choice these changes can be extremely exciting. They can also be tough. In both cases they will challenge that element of personal gravity – familiarity. Before the change you knew where you stood with life and felt some modicum of control over work, relationships and the things that mattered to you most. Now, because someone else says so, one or other of those parameters will have changed.

These changes come most often from the world of work and personal relationships:

■ Work changes: promotion, new team, company merger, losing your business – the possibilities are endless. Sometimes there will have been no way of knowing. Sometimes if you had paid attention you could have prepared yourself or taken action.

■ Personal relationship: this touches the heart of how you see yourself. When you begin a new relationship, the kids leave home or a beloved pet dies, you find yourself re-thinking who you are and how you want to live your life. Again, you may have known in theory what was about to happen, but the reality will feel very different.

Even the most positive of changes challenges your assumptions. Think of falling in love: in those early days nothing can rock your boat – life is fantastic! As the relationship normalises, things you take for granted come up for grabs – after all, who doesn't drop their socks on the floor at night and who ever expected to leave on time for a party!

Successful relationships – work and personal – are those where people are willing to give up on familiarity and look for the ways that work best for everyone.

Going with the flow

Serial achievers are quick to spot restlessness and begin the process of change. Jill, however, never had that luxury. Her husband's job in the air force meant the changes came to her regularly whether she wanted them or not. 'I never stayed in anything long enough to get restless. I would just be climbing the ladder to be head of department or just getting my own business going and we would have to move.'

'It was all the interviews that got to me. I used to get very nervous because it was important I got the job – the air force never paid that well. I just had to keep proving myself to the next employer.'

Jill learned to live with the fact that she wasn't in control of her own future. She embraced the changes by putting her marriage and family first – this enabled her to deal with the upheavals as they arrived. Even though they were not of her choosing, she was never passive. She used her core talent of adaptability and creativity really well, developing her skills until she had built a number of small businesses, taught English as a foreign language, become a head of department in a senior school, set up a computer course that taught the value of spreadsheets and been an advisory teacher.

In the long run, the changes brought her plenty of opportunity to develop the full range of her talent – all of which she uses now in her new business of garden design.

Changes we choose

Now we are in full control, or so it would seem. However, instigating the change doesn't mean full control over how it goes. The unexpected will always occur.

Change is what the life alignment curve is all about. Feeling restless, serial achievers set off to incubate the next steps. At this point, all options are open and they come right up against their assumptions, expectations and desires. This challenge helps them clarify what they want the change to look like and what they need to do to make it happen – then they can deliver when the time is right.

This is exactly what happened to Peter Fisher when he decided to set up his business selling computer hardware. At the outset, it was just a bright idea to help pay for travel to see his in-laws in California. The idea took off pretty much instantly and soon they were packing boxes at night after a full day at work.

'You learn a huge amount about your potential when you run a business. Flying by the seat of your pants, you have to access deeper parts of yourself that you have needed before.' This is just the sort of learning that helps a serial achiever take on the next life chapter – understanding that you have unplumbed depths is a comfort when the challenges pile in.

Often, it is only in retrospect that we see just how positive even the most negative change has been. For example, Robin Millar went through a number of tough changes in his business, yet he has no regrets. Among other benefits, he recognised, 'I am really good at coming up with ideas, making connections and doing deals, but then I need to step back and let someone else take over.'

EXPLORATION

What learning have you taken from the significant changes in your life? Look at the questions below and consider how effective you are in learning from change.

Change	Impact	Learning gained
Name the change ■ Traumatic ■ Came to you ■ Chosen by you	Which area of your personal gravity was affected? What was the main challenge it brought to you? How did you respond – in a positive or negative way?	What did you learn from the change? How has it changed your approach / behaviour? How will you manage this form of change in the future?

Reviewing past change in this way helps mitigate concerns about future change. My guess is that you will see that real learning came out of even the toughest change – not least that you survived!

Once you can see both the challenge and opportunity then you are truly embracing the change and will make the very best of it.

Managing change

As a serial achiever, you will take on significant change many times in your life. Each time you travel through the life alignment curve, you will see a tangible difference – your relationships will adapt and you will re-align your own style to enable you to move with the new direction.

"Each time you will see a tangible difference."

First, you have to spot that change is needed or imminent and then decide how you are going to react.

Spotting the need for change

'When I'm bored with the same routine there is little satisfaction. Waking in the morning and not wanting to go to work lets me know I'm beginning to stagnate, so I start considering my options.' This is how Chris Mullinder knows when he needs a change.

Su Lissanevitch is similar – 'I get restless as soon as work becomes mechanical. I love change, it startles me into learning something new, which is always exciting.'

Both Su and Chris are investigative and move away from dissatisfaction, so the trigger of boredom helps them spot the need for change. They start to look at the possibilities, which bring back interest and excitement to their lives.

Laura Pelling is at the opposite end of the scale. She is introspective and works hard to make the most of a tough situation, learning a huge amount about herself along the way. This is classic behaviour in serial achievers who contain dissatisfaction – restlessness raises its head, but they feel they need to keep trying. Familiarity and life pressure cause them to hesitate until the discomfort gets so bad, they just have to move.

Either way, that time of restlessness and boredom is one of low energy that can leave you feeling depleted if you don't act. Whatever your style, there are two important things that will encourage you:

1. As soon as you embrace the change, you take back responsibility and your energy begins to return.

2. You rehearse change first in your mind, so don't feel that you have to jump to fast action. Thinking and planning can release just as much energy and enthusiasm as the change itself.

EXPLORATION

When boredom or dissatisfaction make themselves felt, undertake a quick review of where you are:

▨ Where is the real area of dissatisfaction

- – personal life?

- – world changes?

- – work situation?

▨ Once you have identified the problem, consider what a great outcome would look like.

▨ If you were to go for 'great' what would this mean you have to

- – do differently?

- – give up?

- – change in other areas of your life?

▨ Which presents a bigger challenge to you at present – maintaining the dissatisfaction or making the required changes?

If containing your dissatisfaction is just too demanding, then you are primed for change and it is time to think through your options and plan your next steps.

However, if it feels hard to give up your present position, then you are probably not quite ready. In which case, all you can do is carry on. Your only action now is to mull over what being ready will look like, so you will spot the moment as soon as it arrives.

Managing change in different ways

Laura contains dissatisfaction because she dislikes sudden change. Taking the process in stages helps her move on, as her last change of job demonstrates. She applied for her boss's job and lost out to an external candidate. However, she was offered an alternative post in the same company that she thought might work. She considered all the implications and decided it was worth a go. 'The job could be interesting and I get a jump in salary. I will do it for one year then when I am more marketable, I can leave if I want to.' The job also had the benefit of being in the same company with the same people.

'So in terms of change, I started to acclimatise myself and the family. After six months in the new job, my son pushed the button – I mentioned that I had a horrible day lined up and he asked me why I was doing it. It was just the right question! I looked at job adverts and saw the job I was going to apply for. I am quite fatalistic – when I am going to make a change, I tend to think the right answer will come to me. I think it's about being open to the opportunity.'

Laura makes her change in stages:

- The desire for change begins almost unconsciously: 'I just know I am going to change.'
- She begins to talk about it to close people she trusts.
- Finally, there is a trigger that shows her it is time for action.

From then on, she relies heavily on gut reaction: 'If something feels bad, I won't do it. This is about values, not about being scary. Change is always a bit scary so I expect that.'

Craig has a different style. He responds well to crisis, enjoying the challenge and excitement. Once his job goes to 'business as usual' he finds it dull, so goes on a hunt for the next problem. This apparent ease with crisis comes from a complex mix of experience and values:

- He navigated a financial family crisis in his adolescent years by earning his own money. He learned that he did well when faced with a problem.
- His irresistible curiosity means he leaves no stone unturned, so he is very good under pressure.

■ He believes in doing the right thing, so his maverick quality is coupled with trustworthiness.

Once Craig has his vision for change, he is relentless in pursuing it. He doesn't let go for a moment: 'I'm like a dog with a bone. I fly all over, drive myself to the point of exhaustion, then launch the new product/vision/business. This is all very exciting, but then anti-climax kicks in and I need my next goal. I can slow down on holiday, but I also let things slip. So pressure and change is how I achieve.'

When change arrives

What you actually do will vary according to where the change comes from.

Acting on changes that come to us

The first action is to take responsibility – you may not have chosen the change, yet how you manage it and what you make of it is entirely up to you.

"What you make of it is up to you."

Murray was doing really well in his work as an IT project manager, so he was soon asked to take on the role of manager. He was delighted with the opportunity and also a bit daunted by the steep learning curve into people management. 'I would have loved to teleport six months on – I don't like not knowing – so I spent my time trying to get a foothold.'

When unexpected change comes your way, any action you take towards that foothold will give you back a sense of control. To do this, you just have to get started:

- Sit back and take a good look at the situation. Which bits are you confident about and where is your real learning edge? Identify what you need to know.

- Never be afraid to ask for help. Whatever you have to take on, someone will have done the same or similar before you. Look at your network and see who you need to talk to.

- Work out a plan of action – it's amazing how comforting this can be! Create the plan in your own style – the point is to realise that you can add value, so you can get alongside the change.

This is just what Murray did at the outset. He worked out what he could do already, then took some expert advice on the new tasks. He read books, talked to his team about what was needed and how they might all work together and then put together his plan. 'The turning point was when people started to come to me as their manager and I felt able to fix things for them or coach them to do it themselves.' Not only is Murray now a very good manager, he knows that he is good at managing new challenges when they hit him.

Acting on changes we choose to take on

When you have instigated the change, you have an idea of where it is going and what you need to achieve, so at least you have a head start. Of course, you are still going into the unknown – so you need to be on your toes.

The people you work with are always something of a wild card. Robin discovered this when he started his own record label. Already very successful in the music business, he failed to take in that he isn't skilled at finding the right people to run the business with him. He got taken in by their debonair ways, which made them fun to be around, but didn't mean they could do the job. As a result, Robin lost that business, but learned what to do differently next time.

When you know the change and have control over the process, keep in mind:

- You can't actually control everything, so keep checking the plan of action to see if it still fits.

- Not everyone will respond to change in the same way you do. Make time to listen to family, friends and colleagues to find out how they are doing and what they need from you.

- Celebrate successes as they arise, so you can enjoy the fruits of your labour!

Allowing change to happen

Managing change doesn't always require you to take direct action – sometimes you just need to let it be.

Imagine for a moment that you have come out at the other end of the incubation period. Whatever happened, you will have learned a great deal about yourself and your new life chapter. Yet, however well you plan the next steps and focus your mind on the new project, things won't fall into place.

This may just be because you haven't yet completed the change. Sure, you are 'acting as if' and doing all the right things. But something doesn't fit. And the something is probably you!

"You need to settle in to who you are now, so you can act authentically."

Every time you go through the life alignment curve, you become slightly different – you learn more about yourself and your core talent, you build different relationships and your attitude to life matures. These are big changes, but much less tangible than setting up a business or learning a skill. You need to settle in to who you are now, so you can act authentically. Unfortunately this can be hard to do if:

- you haven't yet recognised that your personal gravity has changed, so you carry on acting habitually on old assumptions;

- you have been so busy taking action that you've missed just what a big personal change this is;

- you're not ready to see the other changes that might flow from being your new self.

This is all par for the course on the life alignment curve. Whenever you change, you open up new elements of yourself. Until you recognise this aspect of the change, you are discombobulated, just not sure who you are! All you know to do is to carry on the way you were – acting like a student when you have a responsible job, becoming a parent without recognising that your priorities have changed, acting the way you think a 'pensioner' should even though you are spry and lively – these are all ways in which you give away some of your personal power and ability.

So give yourself time to adjust to a change. Think about who you are as a result of your time of learning. This is a paradox – you don't actually have to do anything. Just relax into yourself and you will find the other changes begin to flow.

Where are you now?

As a serial achiever, change is going to be a constant part of your life, so getting to grips with where it comes from and what it means is time well spent:

- You understand where change comes from and how to make the best of it.

- You see how change can help you in your development.

- You know what to do once the changes arrive.

Now you are clearer on change, you can go out and invite opportunity to knock ...

BEHAVIOUR FOUR

Invite opportunity

SERIAL ACHIEVERS LOOK FOR OPEN DOORS – THEY ARE ALWAYS READY TO WALK THROUGH THEM

'It was my final meeting and it didn't feel right to leave without sharing my thoughts for improving women's fashion.' Susan Bull's consultancy work with a large department store chain was finished, but she still felt committed to its success. Their immediate response was: 'OK, so when will you start?' The outcome was a fashion show that she took around the country, showing new and interesting ways of dressing.

By taking her responsibility to the client seriously, Susan also invited more opportunity for herself. She didn't speak out for that reason – in fact, she was getting restless and ready to move on – but they saw her sincerity and heard the sense in what she was saying. By taking on her ideas, they connected to her excitement, so she couldn't resist the challenge. 'I'd never actually done a show on this scale before – I knew I would have to re-invent it for each venue and that made it a fascinating prospect.'

Serial achievers consistently put themselves in the way of opportunity. Sometimes this is conscious effort, sometimes their natural style – like Susan. Either way, their commitment to an end result is what gives them the edge.

Framing the opportunities you want

Remember the section in Behaviour One on luck: 'Trust the lord and tie up your camel'? You can trust that *something* will happen, whatever you do – life is just like that and great things often seem to come out of nowhere. However, you can also increase the chances of that something being positive and make sure you are ready to grab it with both hands.

The first step in inviting opportunity is to train your brain to be on the lookout for the right opening, which means you need a rough idea of your direction, because:

- opportunity is always out there – we are constantly surrounded by possibilities;
- you can only choose from what you see – we restrict what we take in, to avoid being overwhelmed;
- as soon as you focus your mind, it will direct you to the relevant opportunities.

In essence you need to create a mindset about your next life chapter, because mindsets impact directly on how your mind works. The more you focus on an idea, issue or thought, the more your brain looks for opportunities that link to it. So when you are pregnant, the streets are suddenly filled with kids and pregnant women.

"Create a mindset about your next life chapter."

There are two elements to that picture of the future:

- developing a rough idea of the new direction of travel;
- deciding how you want to go about it.

The new direction of travel

Building this picture of the coming chapter is the work of the incubation period. You start the process of focusing your mind, which begins to build the new mindset. The trick is to make it specific, but not too detailed. This sounds like a contradiction – and it is, but there is a very good reason why.

'Beware of what you ask for,' is a phrase we often use when aspirations go wrong. The desire for money is a perfect example. Many people talk hopefully of winning the Lottery in the belief that money will change their lives. Unfortunately, if they are miserable and frustrated before they win, they'll probably still be miserable and frustrated, albeit in a bigger house. The point is that no single factor will deliver a good life – you need a much fuller picture of the future for it to work.

The answer lies in making the picture vague. Just like a watercolour, the overall shape gives you enough of a 'feel' – you recognise it without a need for all the detail. Building your own watercolour keeps your options open for something new and outside your present frame of reference, which is what change is all about.

So the incubation period delivers the focus of your next commitment:

- you go through a time of confusion and uncertainty;
- gradually, what you need starts to come into focus;
- you become highly sensitised and concentrate your energy on the next steps.

The reason for the epiphany is that you have been gradually realigning yourself as the picture emerges. Once you make the final commitment – as long as you haven't put blinkers on by trying to define your specific goals too soon – the next steps appear and you can see opportunities that you were blind to before.

You will get better at this as you move through each life chapter – your 'vision' continues to improve, increasing your ability to see what life presents and ensuring that you are open to new opportunities.

Interestingly, few of the serial achievers in this book had specific goals for their lives. And those that did are still working towards them or accepting that they will probably never happen!

Keeping your options open

I worked with someone recently who heartily disliked the job he was in and wanted desperately to work somewhere else. We talked about the need to build a new mindset and, of course, he focused on the job. One soon came along, which turned out to be just as bad as before.

So he needed to refine the mindset – to create a watercolour of his happy life. This meant considering life overall:

- how he would feel at the end of a good day's work;
- what home life would be like when he felt happy and fulfilled;
- the impact a good salary would have, etc.

Building his watercolour created a balanced picture of what really mattered, taking him away from the artificial focus on one element of his life. Change wasn't immediate, but in time the right job came along and it wasn't at all what he expected. It was different work in a very different sector, but one that was much more satisfying.

The risk in being specific is that you don't know what the best life chapter will be – you may need a more radical change than you can presently imagine. So keep your new mindset general about the next step and specific about your life in the long term and you will be in with a chance of moving in the right direction.

The strange thing about change is that once we accept what we really want – rather than what we think we should want or are scared we need – it becomes effortless and doors start to open.

"Once we accept what we want doors start to open."

EXPLORATION

'I don't believe that wanting things "badly" is the best way, as this gets you tense and all chewed up inside. I think "relaxed proactive" is the best!' This is Andy Wraith's view on getting your mind in the right place for action. It makes sense – as soon as you become tense, you are into worrying – different mindset altogether!

Think about your view of the future. Focus not on the specifics of what you will do, rather on what life will feel like when you are doing the right thing:

- Imagine yourself arriving home in the evening having spent the day doing something that mattered to you – what will that *feel* like?

- How will you talk about your life to people around you – what qualities will you pick to rave about?

- When you take the 'the test of a life well used' which features of this particular life passage will you be proud of?

You will be very tempted to get specific – salary, working hours, amount of holiday. Please resist! The ideal job for you could be totally different – don't back your mindset into a corner.

Write an account of your ideal life or draw the watercolour in your notebook, relating it to your core talent. Remind yourself of the picture regularly so it feels as real as possible. Give your mind the best chance at finding the right options.

Defining your delivery style

Diana Tibble has always been clear about the way she wants to work. During her time as a staff nurse, there was a nursing officer who took exception to her style. He called her 'a people pleaser who can't say No'. At first, it hurt her to hear it, but she now knows that it is the one thing that has made her successful in every field she has entered. 'I took his comment to heart and reflected on it. It helped me to realise that my ability to care so deeply and honour people's suffering is what made me a good nurse. He is right, I do "bend over backwards", and it has given me the most successful homeopathic practice in the area.'

Being a serial achiever is about what you do *and* about how you do it. You can't achieve without other people, so building strong relationships and being trustworthy are big elements of continuing success.

EXPLORATION

You may already have a clear style that you want to stick to, like Diana. If not, give some thought to what that might look like:

- Think of when you have felt happiest about the way you worked and the relationships you had with people in your life. Write down the specifics of how you behaved and why it mattered.

- Consider people you admire and look at how they behave with the people around them – write down some notes to help you explore exactly what it is they do.

- From these two areas of consideration, produce a summary of what your own style of delivery and relationship will be like when you are living the life you want.

This picture of your style will complete your watercolour of the future and will help embed your new mindset.

Behaviours that invite opportunity

Serial achievers are always either working towards their next peak or enjoying that relaxing time of stability before the next challenge comes along. And throughout, they practise the behaviours that invite opportunity – just in case!

Taking opportunities as they arise

Barbara Evans had an early lesson in inviting opportunity from her mother, who had grown up at a time when women had few possibilities open to them. There were many things her Mum would like to have done, including following the family tradition of being a police officer, but by the time she was old enough to join, she was married and in those days, she couldn't do both.

Barbara did follow the long-standing family tradition and got herself a place in the local force. 'Just after I got my letter to say start at the training centre in Warrington, my boyfriend asked me to join him in Australia.' They had met just as he was about to emigrate and had stayed in touch. She went out for a holiday and then he asked her to join him – what timing!

She was totally confused – which should she do? Mum had a very clear answer, 'You are probably only going to get this one chance to go to Australia, so why miss it? You can always come back and pick up later.' An interesting response from someone who had always wanted what Barbara had on offer. She clearly understood the importance of taking up an opportunity when it arose and not backing off a challenge when it comes to you.

'I felt very nervous about it and a bit strange because I had spent twelve months in the application process.' She needn't have worried, it all worked out really well. For most of her time out there, she worked as PA to a property developer – 'it was a different world – quite amazing.' It set her on a work path in facilities management in Australia and UK. Then at the age of forty-eight she finally took up a place as a police officer.

So how do you go about inviting opportunity? The purpose is to open up possibilities that may lead you towards the life you want. The concept of inviting means you have to 'lay out your stall', letting people know who you are and what you have to offer, so they can contact you, if and when the time is right. You also have to open your own mind, so you can spot the opportunities and be ready to 'walk through a door when it opens'.

"Walk through a door when it opens."

Given that you don't know what the opportunities will look like or where they might come from, you need to spread your net wide:

- focus on your core talent;
- make contact with interesting people;
- keep your mind open to new possibilities;
- be helpful;
- let personal experience introduce you to ideas and possibilities;
- say 'Yes' to opportunities when they arise.

Focus on your core talent

This is primarily about opening your mind to your core talent. It can be challenging to 'own up' to talent, so start now to focus on what you do really well:

- Ponder on your core talent, so you understand it fully – you will probably be surprised!
- Review your present work/activities and consider how you can use your core talent more effectively day to day.
- Practise talking in core talent terms. You don't have to go into detail, just let it frame what you say, eg: 'I'm happy to take on that task because I can ...'

This way of thinking keeps your talent in the forefront of your mind. You will be surprised at how much opportunity you begin to see once your mind is on side.

Make contact with interesting people

Serial achievers understand that opportunities arise through people, so they build good relationships. The result is that:

- people remember you and understand where you are coming from;
- you learn about other people, opening your eyes to life outside your own arena;
- you discover new areas of interest through learning about what they do.

The possible outcomes are endless – you make new friends, build great business contacts, stick in someone's mind when they need an expert, learn a skill because someone aroused your interest. Refer back to Behaviour Two for ideas.

Keep your mind open to new possibilities

There is a whole world out there of new ideas, worthwhile information and established knowledge and advice. So keep your mind open to new learning for the interest and possibilities it can bring you.

Opportunity doesn't knock for those who believe they know it all – be flexible, recognising there is always more to learn. You know that phrase – if you don't use it, you'll lose it. So keep your mind as active as you can.

If you don't know where to start, listen to what other people talk about and follow your nose. This is another example of 'trusting the lord' as outlined in Behaviour One – letting life lead you to new possibilities and ideas. You don't have to take them all on – have a taste then make a choice:

- Explore some networking websites – Facebook, LinkedIn, MySpace – all are ways of meeting other people and exploring different ways of connecting.

- Get the programme for your local theatre and just go – never mind if you haven't heard of it before.

- Do something new – trace your heritage, learn to cook, take up archery.

- If you need to refine different behaviours, have a go at Second Life on the web and try them out. You will get feedback and improve as you go along. If it works, just remember to use the behaviour for real – please don't just leave it in the virtual world!

Once you start to think about it, you'll realise there are all sorts of options out there. Your task is to challenge your own thinking by introducing something new. You will soon find that your mind speeds up and the new ideas and events will seem worth the effort.

Helen Hanson used this to great effect. She became interested in jewellery and decided to have a go at it herself. Living in Hong Kong, she had access to specialists in China who were expert at implementing any design, so she put together a small collection. Her friends really liked it and soon she was producing more designs and greater numbers. One friend even took some of her pieces back to a shop owner the UK who found them very easy to sell.

It was all very exciting and she did it for as long as it stayed fun. Given that she had three small children at the time, it was very demanding. Yet it kept her mind on tick-over and added a new string to her bow. And who knows what might happen in the future.

Add value

Gina Coleman does this really well. 'I have always believed I will make my own luck. Even in my Saturday job when I worked in Fenwick's at Brent Cross in the toy department, I looked for ways to give more than was expected. Before long the buyer there gave me the job of Saturday supervisor which meant I had to cash up at the end of the day.'

'I look at how other people work and think of ways I can do the same thing, but better. I've always liked pleasing people – I think it goes back a long way to when my Mother called me and I was half way up the road before I knew what she wanted from the shops!' As a result Gina has held a number of fascinating jobs moving from being PA to a number of chief executives to holding a senior position in public relations.

You will be surprised at how interesting this approach makes life. Take any situation and look at how you can give additional value. People will appreciate your enthusiasm and interest and you will learn more about all sorts of situations.

"Look at how you can give additional value."

Harriet Kelsall learned about this from her maths teacher at school. Janet Goldsmith was challenging and inspiring, and had a big impact on Harriet. She always said: 'There is more than one way to answer a problem – it's up to you how you solve it.' Being helpful gives you a real opportunity to put a problem in a different light and find other solutions.

Let your personal experience introduce you to new ideas

Life will keep offering opportunities for you to consider, you just have to spot them for what they are.

Letting life show you the way

When Diana worked as a nurse, she kept getting infections that the doctors couldn't deal with. A friend suggested that she go to a homeopath, since all she had to lose was £30. 'So I went to see this funny little chap who asked me ridiculous questions and he gave me a silly white pill that was very ethereal – me who is so feet on the ground! Anyway, I haven't had an infection since. It doesn't take much to make me realise – I was totally on board.'

After going through her pregnancies with him and just bouncing back, she began to look into it further. She soon decided to train as a homeopath herself. 'Once I get a bee in my bonnet, I'm a terrier and totally tunnel vision. I see something, look into it, like it and go for it. Nothing will deflect me. It fills me with excitement and I love the challenge.'

Once Diana had qualified she worked as both a homeopath and a midwife until the homeopathy could take over. 'I just went and talked to people about it. I went to twins clubs, women's clubs, all over to talk about it and within a couple of years I had a very busy practice, which is not that common in this field.'

Diana allowed her personal experience to open a new door – she had never heard of homeopathy, but finding it worked for her roused her interest and the rest is history.

You always find opportunities in life if you are prepared to look. Work, home, fun, life with your children – all will show you something new at different times. So follow your nose and you will seemingly 'fall over' a new challenge.

Derek Ffoulkes had a major operation – not quite the opportunity you would hope for. However, he was able to use even this as a spur. 'Life is just too short, so I am more outspoken and challenging now – more real, increasing my ability to make a difference.' This adds significant value to his work as a head of human resources.

It is all about widening your way of thinking. Nothing is one-dimensional – experience the feelings and then stand back and look at it from a different angle, like Derek did.

EXPLORATION

Look back over your life in the past three years and identify *one* event that had a big influence on you:

■ What was your experience of the event? How did you feel about it?

■ What did you think about the experience? Did it all make sense?

■ How did you respond? What was your first action and your subsequent considered actions?

As you think about the event in this way, consider:

■ the main learning you have taken from it;

■ how you are using that learning now in your life;

■ how you might use the learning more effectively in the future.

If you find you haven't learned from the event, give some thought now to what you can take from it for future reference. There is always something that will be of benefit.

Get into the habit of looking at personal experiences in this way in the future. If you notice any spark of interest, be prepared to follow it.

Say 'Yes' to opportunities when they arise

This is a behaviour that will open many doors, not least to understanding just how gutsy you can be!

First let's clarify – never say 'Yes' to something that is illegal or could do you harm. Always take good care of yourself.

What we are talking about are those moments when you say 'No' out of habit. This is the ideal time to question why and experiment with saying 'Yes' instead.

Miriam McLoughlin took this approach on her journey to India. When asked to join her friends in something new and different, she automatically said 'Yes'. This was her way of 'trusting the lord' so she could experience life to the full. However, she had already 'tied up her camel' by finding people she could trust, who knew the country well. As a result, she learned a huge amount, not least that when rats run over her feet at their temple of worship, she can contain herself! Plus her bit part in a Bollywood film brought much fun and a story to dine out on for years to come. Much better than sitting in her lodgings wondering what India was really like!

'Just get on and do it!'

Robin Millar knew he had to get noticed if he was to make his way in the music industry. Never one to back off a challenge, he was constantly on the lookout for opportunities.

Through the grapevine he heard about a recording studio that had fallen on hard times. Never having done a business deal before, he joined forces with a friend who helped put together a business plan to take to venture capitalists. 'The first one turned us down – he said you can't have a blind person running a business. That just made me more determined to do it. I saw ninety VCs and number ninety gave me the money!'

Challenges remained, but finally he persuaded the owners to sell to him and set about improving the place. At the suggestion of a young publicist, he not only rented out the studio space, he used it to make records that he would own.

A major result from that particular 'Yes' was being sent a tape by a funky band called Pride. 'I listened to it at 3am one morning and realised that if I could produce this singer I would have cracked it. I called them the next day. We spent one week together producing two songs that set us all on our way.' The singer was Sade and the songs, 'Smooth Operator' and 'Your Love is King'.

Robin discovered over time that the first venture capitalist had been right – it is hard to run a business when you can't see the books and contracts.

However, that hasn't stopped him taking on opportunities when he sees them: 'If you have a really good idea, at least six other people will have had it too. So just get on and do it!'

The ability to say 'No' is important and necessary; saying 'No' out of habit is an unnecessary restriction. What we are looking for here is an open mind, willing to try new experiences. I guarantee you will find yourself to be more resourceful, resilient and able than you have ever thought. You will gain in self esteem and open up new doors of opportunity.

EXPLORATION

It is important to understand how you stop yourself, so next time you are invited to be part of something new and different, think about the following:

- When you say 'No', notice what stops you. What are you concerned about?
- What is the risk of saying 'Yes'? Is it dangerous or just embarrassing? What are you really afraid of?
- Imagine yourself saying 'Yes.' What does that feel like?

If you find this was a habitual 'No', then you have a choice. Tie up your camel by checking the situation – do you trust the people involved, eg does the bungee jump organisation follow safety rules?; are you with people who will look out for you? If so, then manage your own concerns and give it a go.

Saying 'Yes' to yourself

The thing to understand about opportunity is that it is always there. It is tempting to hold on to past success for fear that nothing more will follow. This is absolutely not true – unless you choose it that way.

The big rule for serial achievers is to go for the peak and move on. Let go of the assumption that there is a limit to what you can achieve – there are as many peaks as you want and are willing to work for. This requires you to give up on all the limiting assumptions you make about yourself:

- I'm too old now.
- I'm not clever enough.
- I can't do it because I'm a woman/black/disabled.

All these statements originate in the drag of personal gravity. It is mindsets and familiarity at play, attempting to keep you safe and out of harm's way. The risk is that they put you into the way of boredom, underachievement and regret.

EXPLORATION

Next time you have a moment of self doubt, consider the two aspects of personal gravity:

- Drag: long-standing mindsets that have served you well. They hold you in familiar situations so you don't put yourself at risk. They may be keeping you safe or they may be holding you back.

- Lift: these may be long-standing mindsets or new ones formed as a response to recent life passages. They work to drive you towards new experiences and learning. They may provide you with real opportunity or they may be reckless and put you at risk.

Your task in this exploration is to explore both sides and decide which one serves you in the present situation. Identify a recent choice and look at your messages of drag and lift – remember either one can be positive or negative.

Situation	Drag	Lift
Offer of a job in a new arena	At my age, I should settle down

I will need to sort out my pension

Everyone will know more than me

It will be hard work but I can do it | It will be boring – I'll know more than everyone else

There will interesting people to meet

I can do better than this!

What a lot I will learn! |

Once you have thought it all through, decide which aspect you want to go with. Use this process next time an opportunity presents itself.

Throughout this book there are examples of people who are older, female, black, disabled, who don't believe they are clever, had bad starts in life – and they are all very much serial achievers. So take the limitation off yourself and say 'Yes' to the best you can be – today and the year after that. As long as you are alive you have a core talent and there are plenty of opportunities out there to use it.

"Take the limitation off yourself and say 'Yes' to the best you can be."

Where are you now?

Hopefully, you're having a good time saying 'Yes' to a few more interesting opportunities! In addition, you will be working on:

■ developing your own exciting watercolour for the next steps and building a real understanding of how you want to go about it;

- starting to embed the behaviours in your day-to-day life and spotting opportunities as they approach you;
- trusting that there are more peaks ahead of you yet and enjoying experimentation.

Let's look now at what drives you to action and how to go about it . . .

BEHAVIOUR FIVE

Be passionate

SERIAL ACHIEVERS ARE PASSIONATE – THEY CHANNEL THEIR PASSION INTO ACTION

Lucy Shuker shouldn't be able to play wheelchair tennis as well as she does. As a high paraplegic she has no core muscles to help her stay in the chair as she reaches out for a ball, so competing against an amputee who can use her whole body is a tough ask. However, when you factor in Lucy's passion for the game and for making the most of her life, then you begin to see how she does it.

She has always pushed against the norm, even before her accident – which is just as well, given how hard she has to fight to continue with her tennis. There is no funding, other than a small Lottery grant that kicked in when she became No 1 in the UK. She has to go to a particular gym to be able to train; travel around the world for competitions to keep up her ranking; and raise the funds alongside to make it all possible.

Without a deep passion for the sport and determination to have a quality life, it is hard to see why she would go on. But then passion drives all serial achievers. Whether passion for a cause, money, family, the work itself – there is always that measure of excitement that makes it all worthwhile.

Passion – or the lack of it – also explains why restlessness can suddenly set in. There is nothing like working in an arena that excites and inspires you. It builds energy all on its own and you achieve beyond your wildest dreams. Having such a wonderful time also makes it hard to carry on when the flame has gone out. Once the desired outcome is achieved, it is time to move on to something that gets the spark going again.

This is the story of serial achievement: do work that matters – for as long as it matters – then move on.

"Do work that matters – for as long as it matters – then move on."

The magic of working with passion

Anna Smółka was managing director of the Polish Newspaper Association in the early 1990s. It was a time of adventure and true passion for building something of meaning out of the difficult years of Communism.

Her role gave her the opportunity to co-operate with a small group of people who were determined to build an influential newspaper that would contribute to a positive future for Poland. 'These people were friends, sitting in one room in old pullovers, smoking cigarettes – that was the moment some of them started to be politicians and some started to be very important journalists.' Driven by a passion for their people and their country, they set out to found the company Agora and the influential newspaper *Gazeta Wyborcza*.

As the company became successful, interesting new people were brought in to work with the 'elders', who were keen to convey that this wasn't just a newspaper that earned money. 'They told the newcomers that this is a newspaper that changes our world and our lives. We fight for something that is important to all of us – a new world for Poland.'

Driven by their passion for Poland, these people took action by working crazy hours, often until 2am in the morning. The paper was – and still is – a success, but the impact on the people who created it has been varied:

■ Some worked so hard they were broken by the effort. They were rewarded well, which turned out to be a mixed blessing – the lack of money worries meant they had no reason to look for the next challenge. Life became depressing and lacking in passion.

- Some stayed in the company and adapted to working in a successful business producing the standard daily papers. 'They do well, but it is no longer so wonderful.'

- Others used their money to set up a new challenge – something very different that they could get excited about. By focusing on a new passion they found a way to direct their energy and achieved great success.

A huge amount was achieved by these people – Anna included – because they contributed their full passion and commitment. It is a great example of how enlivening and exciting it is to work with passion and how important to move on to something new when the time is past. Once you know what it is like to use your passion fully, everything else pales into insignificance.

Experiencing such a passion for life is amazing. People who live through extreme conditions have to put everything into survival, because they are fighting for the life they knew or the life they want in the future. They show us just how much can be achieved through a deep passion.

For some, this time of inspiration comes just once in their lives – they have one major peak, then keep trying to repeat it rather than moving on. Their energy begins to stagnate and all they can do is look back. The episode where they lived day by day with their passion becomes 'the best years of my life' because nothing before or since has ever matched up.

This is the recipe for years of regret, knowing there is more and not being able to access it.

What is passion?

In this context, passion is the strong desire to make a difference and it engages people at an emotional level. When you are passionate, you really care and will do whatever it takes, because it matters.

In contrast, when something makes sense on a rational level, you are prepared to put in time and effort, but it can be difficult to stay focused. It makes good sense, but you don't necessarily feel strongly about it.

I know it makes sense to do the washing up, but I'm not passionate about it, so it feels like a chore. Recycling waste is a different matter – I really believe we need to take more care of the earth, so I will quite happily sort waste into different bins.

So passion links to beliefs and is heartfelt. You are most likely to get passionate about:

- doing work that makes you feel good – like Dave Pack and his music;
- a cause that matters to you – like Naaz Coker working for the Refugee Council;
- supporting people that matter – like Jill Black taking on a job, because her family needed her to and she is devoted to their wellbeing.

Passion also links to core talent. Dave, Naaz and Jill use their talents to deliver and this enables them to go the extra mile. Working in a style that is at odds with your core talent will take all your energy, leaving little enthusiasm for anything more.

So passion together with core talent delivers energy and commitment, making everything easier to achieve.

The pathway of passion

We all know about the passion of falling in love and are fascinated by it – endless movies catalogue that excitement and total commitment to the other person. It is quite possible to feel a similar passion in other areas of life. Serial achievers love that total focus. They have learned that acting with passion is just so much more exciting and rewarding – and once discovered, they never want to work any other way.

Just like a love affair, passion for life follows a set path:

- The first flush of excitement – This is exactly what I want. I feel I can make a real difference.

- Getting going and feeling daunted – Will I be good enough? Will someone discover that I can't really do it? I don't want to let anyone down.

- Total absorption – feeling more confident, taking a few risks, enjoying every moment.

- Normalising the process – a bit less exciting now, day-to-day activities that have to be done, feel it is worthwhile so putting in the time even when a bit bored.

- Overfamiliarity – the project is completed, enthusiasm is running out, so time to liven up the process *or* look for the next challenge.

In relationships, we have to manage the inevitable moment when life becomes predictable. There is no avoiding it, but lots of ways to address it. It is just the same with a life passion, so serial achievers pay attention to energy levels and consider how they need to respond:

- Do I need to identify the problem and refocus?

- Or is it a sign that this life chapter is over and I need to move on?

It can be either. Serial achievers can stay in the same activity for a long time by extending their reach and widening their sphere of influence. Like Tunde Banjoko, who set up and continues to work in LEAP. He keeps it exciting by changing what he does – regular speaking gigs are the latest way of improving the reach of the service, giving him an interesting new challenge.

Fostering passion

Romantic passion can hit you when you least expect it – which is part of its excitement. Passion for life is different – it is more likely to be something that grows from an experience or event.

"Passion for life grows from an experience or event."

Naaz had spent her life believing that her colour wasn't relevant – she was so focused on achieving at work that it wasn't on her radar. Then, a number of events changed her mind, like realising that the white people in her department were socialising without including her. She didn't want to be paranoid, so it was only when she was in a meeting and heard shocking language about black and Indian doctors that she really believed it was true. 'I had been so busy being whiter than white that I neglected who I was and neglected the discrimination that people like me had been suffering. As I became more aware, I realised that my black friends were being treated worse than me, since I could pass as white in the dark, as someone actually told me.'

This was the moment that racism became a passion for Naaz. 'Once I am confident about taking something on, I don't go in for half measures. I talked about it every place I could. I took it fully on board and I still challenge people – but I've learned to do it with charm rather than aggression.'

Dick Pyle is rational by nature, so he doesn't necessarily think of himself as someone who gets passionate about life and work.

Yet he does get deeply involved and firmly believes that 'if you're not going to enjoy what you do, you will never do it well'.

This belief has been reinforced by his experience of doing a job he didn't enjoy and that didn't matter to him. 'I needed a job, so took on some bits of consultancy. The idea was to go into businesses with a clean sweep to help them identify next steps. It was pretty turgid and I'm sure it wasn't my best work!' In contrast, when Dick was running a restaurant, he loved it and was very successful.

Dick speaks of enjoyment rather than passion, yet the essence is the same – he becomes completely engrossed, committing all the energy his project needs.

EXPLORATION

Your first task is to identify what you feel passionate about.

Think about your life at this point in time. Take an average month and list out the activities you are involved in – work, social, hobbies, family, etc. Write the list in a table as below and outline the reasons why you love this particular area of your life or why you are not fully engaged.

Elements of your life, eg:	Reasons for feeling passionate	Reasons for not engaging
Job		
Social		
Child-focused		
Charity work		
Sport/hobbies		

By looking at your own life right now, you will find either:

■ You love what you do – in which case, consider how you can up your game to make the most of your passion.

■ You are not passionate about your work – other areas of your life may keep the interest and enthusiasm high. That may be enough or it may signal a change of direction.

■ You are not passionate about work, but you are passionate about what it brings you, eg it enables you to care for your family really well – and you are passionate about them, so you are fully committed.

Once you have this clarity you know where to focus your attention. Bringing passion into your life is an important part of being a serial achiever.

You and your passion

When passion for life hits, how do you feel? Becoming truly committed to something will take over your life, at least for a time. You will:

■ be totally focused so other aspects of life pass you by entirely;

■ become one-dimensional and tedious to anyone not involved;

■ lose track of time when involved with your passion;

■ turn every other discussion round to fit into your way of thinking;

■ lose sleep because you are so engrossed.

Not only is this all-encompassing for you, it will have a huge impact on the people around you. Imagine living with someone who is totally absorbed in what they are doing! At the first hint that your family, friends or support people are getting fed up, pause to look at the situation from their point of view – how might you help them manage your passion? And as soon as you can, talk it through, listen to their experience, help them understand yours and look for solutions together.

EXPLORATION

BEHAVIOUR FIVE – BE PASSIONATE

As a serial achiever you need backup and support – especially when you get deeply involved in something new. You will also have friends and family around you who need attention. For this reason is it worthwhile understanding your 'downfall' behaviours, ie how you operate when your passion becomes all-consuming and drives others to distraction.

Think about what you are like when totally committed and passionate. Write down a description, in two columns.

Behaviours that benefit relationships	Behaviours that damage relationships
For example:	For example:
Involving backup and support people	Leaving your close family and friends out of the loop
Explaining the benefits and risks to friends and family	Never taking time out for rest and relaxation
Keep outside life going alongside work	Taking risk without due care
Sharing your enjoyment so others are inspired to help you	

If you are not sure, talk to a supporter. This could require a moment of deep honesty as you take in the feedback – they may say you use your passion well or that you get over-involved, messing up other areas of your life. Whatever they tell you, take it seriously and think about how you can make best use of your energy without causing harm elsewhere.

Wearing passion on your sleeve

Susan always had a real passion for fashion. It speaks to her core talent and has provided a lifetime of interest, activity and work.

After leaving school, she went to an art college but it just wasn't right, so she dropped out and looked for a job. Her first port of call was the Brook Street recruitment agency:

'I had on my C&A copy of a Courrèges coat, my black patent shoes and my bomb hat. I was seventeen at the time. With no qualifications, all the person could offer was work in a post room, but she said, 'I'd like you to go and meet this lady – tell her that Fay sent you. So I went to the address and asked for Mrs McRobbie – it turned out that Fay was her daughter.'

Mrs McRobbie was the manageress of Rembrandt Dresses, a fashion house owned by Ellis and Goldstein and she took Susan on as a receptionist. 'It was all because of the way I dressed. I stayed there until I was twenty-two and in that time went from receptionist to manager of the Louis Feraud Collection, which they had brought into the company. This is where I served my apprenticeship in fashion.'

Susan announced her passion to the world through the clothes she wore and it helped her embark on her life path. It is a perfect example of inviting opportunity by showing clearly what your passion is – putting out a marker so like-minded people can spot you.

Linking your passion to action

Just as with your core talent – if you are alive, you are capable of passion. But being passionate is not enough – you need to do something with it

While taking action is exciting, it can also be pretty scary. When you really care, failure feels dreadful. You want so much to do a good job, yet you can only do your best – which may or may not be enough.

To help with this, review your attitude to risk (First Fundamental) and remind yourself that there is no progress without mistakes. In fact, mistakes can often be a turning point into something new and very effective!

There are three elements to take into account when taking action:

- the issues and concerns that matter to you;
- your style of action;
- desire for the output.

Issues and concerns that matter to you

Think about subjects that you discuss at great length or the thoughts and issues that disturb your sleep. They may relate to family and friends, your local community or global issues.

Once you know what matters to you, think about what you do. Do you take action or just talk about it over coffee or a drink with friends? If the latter, then it might be worth revisiting the challenge grid in the Fifth Fundamental – passion without action leaves you in the focused/lethargic box. You may not be fully committed, the issue may not connect to your core talent or you may be coming out of an incubation period and are not yet ready for action.

If you are committed to take action, it helps if you:

- Define the specific area you want to act on – making sure it is something you can do. Think of Tunde – he can't affect the economic climate, but he can help forty people focus their minds on getting a job.

- Work out a first-level plan of action to start you moving – include a thorough review of the possibilities, so you can find the aspect that fits with your core talent.

- Think through your networks – look for like-minded people, or those who know like-minded people, and ask for support or involvement.

- Get your backup and support people to help you think through your plan, support you as you take action and ask those tough questions that are so useful.

Remember to review your plan as you move forward. What you need to do will change as you go, just as the people you need to speak to and involve will change.

Robin Millar has always been passionate about facing up to prejudice, so when he had the opportunity to put his core talent and network to good use, he jumped at it. Some friends from the Chilean Solidarity Group wanted to put out a record on the tenth anniversary of Pinochet's rule to draw attention to their cause. Robin offered them free studio time to do it. He also used his contacts to put together a group of musicians and asked Richard Branson to release it.

We don't all have such powerful networks, but the point is well made. My guess is you know more people than you think you do – or can at least connect to more. It is much easier to sell an idea that you are passionate about, so don't be shy – get out there and ask people to help. You will be amazed at how much support you receive.

"You know more people than you think you do."

Your style of action

You will have your own way of taking action, so make sure you understand what it is. This will be a huge help when you come to address your passion of the moment. It will keep you fully engaged and help you manage the people who want a say in what you do – which may or may not be useful.

The first step in determining your style of action is to explore your core talent – being clear what you have to offer will enable you to make greatest impact.

Think about your particular style and how you can use it to good advantage:

- If you are introverted, look for ways of acting that give you time alone to think and prepare.

- If you are extroverted, make good use of your networking and talk to people who can help you refine your thinking.

- If you enjoy novelty, be prepared to have more than one project, each at a different stage of development.

- If consistency is most comfortable for you, work out a long-term plan that identifies when you need real bursts of energy so you can pace yourself.

Stepping out. The biggest question is whether you will take action at all. Realising you are passionate about something is one thing. To take action is something else altogether. This is the moment where fear and dream must collide – unless you are willing to take the risk of failing, you can't move anywhere.

This is a defining moment – will you risk your dream falling around your ears or do you prefer to keep it pristine and untried? The active step is to embrace the fear and get on with it.

Serial achievers accept this moment of collision. They know it is the only way to find the right action or life chapter. It calls into play personal gravity on a major scale – every mindset will shout loudly about safety versus delight. If you feel at all tempted to back away and give up, return to the test of a life well used: How will you feel when you look back over your ninety years – will you regret not taking this step?

Level of desire

The test of a life well used faces that all-important question – do you want it enough? Change is never easy, even when you are passionate. You have to face challenge, failure, tough times or rejection. Yet all of this will pale into insignificance if you really want something – when your passion is high, nothing will stop you.

"When your passion is high, nothing will stop you."

This is how Dave Pack feels about music. His introverted nature means making the right connections is a challenge, yet he keeps going. 'I know that if I don't push myself, I will regret it – I have to see where this will take me.'

It is passion that carries you through those tough times. If you don't want something enough, however nice the idea, you will always find reasons to procrastinate. Focus where your interest lies and you will have the joy of success and achievement – so much better than a faint hope that was a good idea at the time!

When the passion diminishes

Passion fuels your core talent when you are really committed. Harriet Kelsall knows she can't focus without passion, it is what makes her work so interesting. She loves building a design with someone, giving them exactly the piece of jewellery they want. She does have a bit of a love/hate relationship with it – not everything is a pleasure – yet she pushes herself to action, trusting she will like it once she gets going.

James Nathan learned about the need for passion the hard way – by taking on work that didn't particularly suit him. MasterChef helped confirm just how important cooking is for him and now he is making his way in a world of his own choosing. Yet even when it is just what he wants, there are still down times – spend too long on cold starters and work will soon begin to pall!

Keep following your interest

Mark finally decided to retire from football at the age of thirty-five. For years he had accepted that injury was an inevitable downside of such a thrilling game. But then he found himself playing at a lower level with kids half his age and the shine started to dim.

One match he lost his front teeth and then, in the very next game, he tore his hamstring really badly. On holiday in the south of France with his wife, he finally decided he wasn't enjoying football enough any more.

He realised that once his interest was gone, he lost focus, which meant he no longer wanted to train – something he always used to enjoy. The passion had really gone out of it. All of which would make him more vulnerable to injury, never mind feeling a bit bored. So he accepted it was time to move on with his life, leaving football behind. Now he is running his own business and being a very active father, both of which give him plenty of opportunity to use his passion and core talent.

It is tremendously hard to accept that something you loved for so long is past its sell-by date. Not only are you giving up an erstwhile passion, you face a major change in your life. Both of which can feel quite daunting. So how do you know when it is time to cut your losses?

EXPLORATION

Answer the following questions, giving yourself a rating out of 10 for each one: 10 = absolutely; 1 = not at all.

	Score 1–10
I feel positive each morning, looking forward to the day	
I have lots of new ideas for next steps	
I feel I am achieving something of worth	
Other people are excited to hear about what I'm doing	

	Score 1–10
I am working with like-minded people who feel as passionate as I do	
I really believe in what I am doing	
Total out of 60	

If you score less than 40 it is time to have a good hard look at what you are doing. As a serial achiever, you may be feeling restless and ready for your next life chapter. You may also have gone a bit sleepy on a task that has life in it yet, so spend some time focusing on possible options.

Where are you now?

Finding your passion is enlivening and using it every day is the very best way to live:

■ you have explored your passion and have ideas of how to make the most of it;

■ knowing your style will give you clues about how to go about it;

■ you will know to check out when passion wanes to see what you need to do.

Now it is time to think about making the most of that passion . . .

BEHAVIOUR SIX

Be conscious

SERIAL ACHIEVERS ARE ALERT TO THEIR SURROUNDINGS – THEY WANT TO LEARN FROM EXPERIENCE

Simon Duffy loves to stretch himself. At school, he never felt he was particularly good at anything, yet always took the opportunity to try. Pole vault was one of his regulars. Each year on sports day he volunteered to be the house representative – no one else would do it. One year, he even got over!

He has long recognised the learning that comes from frustration. Never good at writing or explaining, he struggled to be clear in his management work, then had a realisation. 'What I thought I was bad at is, in fact, the thing I do best. Thinking in pictures means I can conceptualise graphically, which makes it easier for a lot of people to understand.' By being conscious and sticking with the frustration, Simon learned about his core talent and has used it to great effect ever since.

Serial achievers take their learning from many different places. By staying conscious of *how* things are happening as well as *what* is happening, they mine the seam of everyday learning to the full. This enables them to refine their behaviour and skills as necessary and ensures they keep growing towards their next life chapter.

Learning and passion

Real learning is driven by passion. Think of a time when you lapped up information or skill training – my guess is you felt really committed to the outcome. That fantastic feeling of being in the right place at the right time helps you motor forward with energy and excitement.

As a serial achiever, being conscious of what matters to you and sticking with it will make learning a joy – even when you are really challenged. Because you want the outcome, you will be prepared to put in time and effort to gain the necessary skills. Whatever is required you will do it with good will and high commitment because it takes you on the path to your next achievement.

Attitude to learning – your personal gravity

Learning experiences in early life leave all of us with personal gravity that provides the lift we need or drags us down into the mire. You might have a motto like Su Lissanevitch that says 'You can do anything you want to do.' Or you may choose to make the best of a familiarity statement that says you are 'not academic, but will get by on your personality' – like Gina Coleman.

As long as your personal gravity acts as a lift, then hold on to it. If your mindsets say you are not OK, then it is time to reframe them into something more positive that will enable you to use your core talent to good effect.

Dropping those old stories

Diana Tibble held on doggedly to the idea that she was thick. It took a presentation to a group of professional hypnotists to finally persuade her otherwise.

'I received a call from one of my trainers, asking me to talk to the British Society of Clinical and Academic Hypnosis on hypnosis and childbirth. This was the pukka place to belong and I wasn't qualified enough to be part of it. I said 'Yes' because my ego loved it, but was soon thinking

'What am I doing!' I had seven months to stew over it and two months before, called up to say I couldn't do it. The organiser told me not to be ridiculous – that of course I was going to do it.'

Diana agreed to keep going – never having backed away from a challenge before. Ten days before, she was having palpitations, feeling genuine fear and anxiety at the prospect of making a fool of herself. 'Then I thought, "healer, heal thyself." I did what I tell my mothers to do when they prepare for giving birth – "Imagine you are going on to a stage and looking at all the people you have given power to. Now find a way to reclaim the power you need to give birth to your baby." So I went through the same process and took back the power I needed to make this presentation. I also told myself I was a competent woman – something I have never managed to do before!

'Well I did it and I felt fab! One chap at the back, a fatherly GP type, came up to me and said, "I just want to tell you that those three people sat at the back are the bods of this society and they said that these are the sort of presenters we want more of." I gave him a kiss! Coming away, I felt I had shed something really significant.'

What a great exercise! Try it yourself when taking on a challenge. If you feel you have too much drag in your personal gravity, take back the power you have given to others in your life. Then you can move on with all your own power at your disposal.

"Take back the power you have given to others."

It certainly worked for Diana. She has since done a second presentation to the BSCAH and been invited to join. So now she is 'pukka' too!

Personal gravity defines how we approach our lives and has a major impact on our ability and willingness to learn.

■ Naaz Coker always enjoyed learning and takes each new challenge on board. 'Whatever I do, I want to do it well.' Her belief in her ability to study gives her a real 'lift' and enables her to gain a deep understanding of each new situation. When taking on her role as chair of the Refugee Council, she read everything she could find on human rights and that gave her the confidence she needed to take action.

■ Harriet Kelsall's personal gravity was very different. She struggled at school, needing the sustained support of her father. About ten years ago she discovered she is dyslexic, which made sense of the problems she'd had. Whatever the reason, the experience taught her a huge amount about her ability to focus and work really hard when she needed to. So she made good use of the tough start – rather than giving into the potential 'drag', she values her difference. What began badly gave her a driver for success and led to a first class honours degree in industrial product design.

■ Peter Fisher only got one E grade at A-level because he chose subjects that didn't fit his core talent of communication, stopping an early move into social work. Instead, he joined Littlewoods as a trainee manager for a year, then took on twelve-hour shifts putting foam rubber on the back of carpets, a lesson in understanding how many people earned their living. Finally, he applied for a job as a house parent at a boys' remand home. Here, he worked with a very experienced housemaster, Graham Granville. 'He knew just how to manage the kids, "Firm, fair, friendly control" – that taught me a lot.' Having learned from his father, as they made transistor radios and intercoms together, Peter knows the value of finding good mentors and emulating what they do well. It is a style of learning that has stood him in good stead over the years.

These three examples show that we each have mindsets about learning that can be used to help or hinder. All these people had tough moments in their education, yet all have taken lessons forward into their adult life.

EXPLORATION

Life learning comes in many different forms, so understanding how you help or inhibit yourself can leave you free to take up opportunities as they present themselves.

Look back over the significant learning experiences in your life to date, choosing the ones that had greatest effect. Note down each one as set out below, thinking about:

- What it taught you – how you interpreted the experience and how it affected your behaviour.

- The impact this made on your personal gravity – what you took from the experience as a 'golden rule' that you still adhere to and whether that rule is positive and gives you 'lift' or is negative and 'drags' you back.

- Decide if this is a rule you wish to continue with. If not, how might you reframe it to a positive?

Let's take Harriet as an example:

Learning experience	Significant lesson	Effect on personal gravity	Keep or reframe?
Struggling at school because of dyslexia Recognising her high IQ	I have to work very hard to get anywhere I am bright enough to do it	Mindset about always working hard Mindset that she can do it	Keep: gets things done and achieves well Reframe: can't let herself relax; can work too hard

For Harriet, the mindsets give her 'lift' so she works hard and can achieve pretty well anything she wants to. The 'drag' element is the difficulty in knowing when to stop, so she can end up exhausted. To reframe it she could, for example, congratulate herself for the work done and take time out as a reward.

Once you have worked through your own learning experiences:

■ Look for the 'lift' and see how you might utilise it more.

■ Consider the areas of 'drag' – make a clear statement of the mindset, eg, I have to work hard and it is not OK to relax. Then turn the statement around into a positive, eg, I will work hard and then enjoy my relaxation.

■ Apply the new positive mindset to present situations and be thrilled when you achieve it!

Where learning comes from

It is tempting to assume that learning comes through reading books or going on a course. An awful lot does, but there's also much to be said for the University of Life – some of the best learning comes from what we do and consciously reflecting on the experience.

Great learning comes from:

■ mistakes and frustration;
■ teachers;
■ life experience;
■ negative examples;
■ challenges.

Mistakes and frustration

Chris Mullinder became deeply frustrated when he worked in a sales company for a few years. He had a standard sales agreement of basic salary plus commission and since Chris is naturally a good salesperson, all was going well. 'I was a victim of my own success – having worked really hard to bring in two large accounts I was told I that I could only have half of the agreed commission!' The rationale was that a national manager, not Chris, did this sort of deal.

Inevitably that was the beginning of the end for Chris. It was a bitter experience, but he learned the skill of forming clear agreements and to look for organisations with integrity.

Most people will have an experience of frustration and learning from mistakes somewhere in their history. It is never an easy memory and can reverberate, if you let it. Recognising the learning value in these difficult situations is a great way to forgive and let them go. As Andy Wraith has found, 'even a wrong decision will open up new opportunities – it is all relative.'

The most difficult mistakes to hear about are those that relate to personal behaviour. No one wants to hear that they have behaved inappropriately, so it needs a moment of deep honesty. Use your listening skills to the full, biting back the instinctive justification, until you understand the impact you made. Only then will you understand what you need to do differently in the future.

"Use your listening skills to the full … until you understand the impact you made."

Teachers

Teachers come in all shapes and sizes – all you have to do is be on the lookout for them. Sometimes you need formal teachers to train you in a new skill, like Jill Black when she decided to learn garden design. 'It was brilliant to use my brain again, learning all the names of the plants. I was the oldest in the class! I'm still in touch with most of them, so made new friends too.'

Yet courses are not the only places to find great teachers. Any parent will tell you that children teach you more about yourself and the world than any degree or qualification! They will:

- reflect back your own behaviour – demonstrating *exactly* how you come across;

- use your own words back to you – so you are left in no doubt about how you sound;

- challenge your resolve – showing how strongly you believe in what you say;

- ignore you at your most pompous – highlighting how quickly you lose touch, when on a roll;

- invite you to play – letting you see how much you allow or suppress your fun side.

So for all you work returners, wondering if you dare to move back to the world of work, remember you have just spent a number of years in 'life school' learning the skills of multi-tasking and managing charming and difficult people!

Role models of any sort are also great teachers. Look out for people you admire, who are doing what you would like to do or who stand out as having qualities you want to develop. Observe what they do that appeals to you. You may even want to be brave and ask for their help. It is lovely to hear that you are admired and most people will respond positively to such a call for help.

Life experience

Susan Bull believes she has learned most from experience. Having spent time in fashion houses, owned a number of shops and worked in design, she now has her own style of relating to customers. 'If I had had this knowledge when I opened my first shop all those years ago I would have done it very differently. No regrets though, because until you do it, you don't understand.'

Years of helping all types women make the most of themselves has crystallised her own theories and she now provides simple rules for anyone to follow. It is a great skill, refined and honed through years of experimentation and learning.

It is a lovely moment, realising that you have enough experience under your belt to be really good in your chosen arena. It comes from taking time to learn from each event:

- understand the positives so you can repeat and improve them further;
- accept the mistakes and analyse them so you can put them right and spot them in the future;
- recognise 'business as usual' for the value it brings you in terms of everyday experience.

Learning from experience can easily be dismissed as 'navel-gazing' – which of course, it is! There are only two problems with navel-gazing:

- not doing enough of it, just repeating the same mistakes over again, being a really slow learner;
- doing so much of it that you fail to put the learning into action.

Believing you can manage without reflection is a great way to keep yourself rooted to the spot. Serial achievers know this won't work – they want to use the opportunity of learning from their experience so they can carry it forward to their next life chapter, building from one life alignment curve to another.

Finding new outlets for experience

Dick Pyle always wanted to retire to France. The time was right – his stock market research work could easily be done online – and he soon found the ideal property. He had also been thinking of a business – 'adopt a truffle tree'. The local farmer agreed to sell a small piece of land that turned out to be perfect for growing truffles. The whole venture was a risk – new country, new idea, new business, but Dick loves a challenge and has masses of experience as an entrepreneur to call on.

The idea captured the imagination of TV and then Neiman Marcus, the department store for people who have everything – except a truffle tree! Now the truffles have adoptive parents in the US as well as Europe.

It was a bit of a gamble, but suited Dick, who enjoys risk. He loves the stimulus of something so new and plans to expand the truffle empire as far as he can.

Negative examples

You won't always know what you want – until you see what you don't want. Mark Barnard experienced this when moving to a new company. He admired the business acumen and drive of the leader, but recognised that he was also overbearing. 'From working with him, I realised how fine the line is between confidence and arrogance.'

Peter Fisher had a similar experience working in an assessment centre, where the leader was totally rule bound. The end result was that everyone became institutionalised – kids *and* staff – and it cost the leader in respect. It provided Peter with great learning and when he needed to employ people for his own business, he looked for those who wanted more than just a job. 'When people feel they can contribute without restriction, there are no barriers to what you can do in a business.' Knowing what the alternative looked like – limited, constrained and soulless – helped him to see what he wanted to do.

Experiences like that help define your own personal style and intention. Both Mark and Peter knew what they didn't want, so ran their own businesses very differently. Anti-role models are just as useful as the positive versions!

Challenges

Taking on a new challenge requires you to pull out all the stops. It can lead to sleepless nights wondering if it is possible or if you will be found out – and a few heart-stopping moments when you feel as if you can't go on. Yet the learning created is enormous. You will learn:

- new skills as you master the challenge;
- just how far your core talent can take you;
- how far you can go with risk and how well you manage in demanding situations.

The nature of challenge is that you go into unfamiliar territory and have to think on your feet. Your core talent will automatically come to the fore and help you negotiate the choppy waters.

"Your core talent will help you negotiate the choppy waters."

Tunde faces challenge every day in his work at LEAP. The programme is designed to help people back to work – people who are out of the routine of early morning starts and consistent attendance. Tunde and his staff would do them no favours by accepting less than the most appropriate behaviour. They provide the opportunity to practise working each day, coupled with a realistic response to poor attendance and punctuality.

Challenge people in this way and they will inevitably challenge back! Being tough with good intention is the rule of the day and Tunde has learned to do this well. Taking each situation on its merits, the team work out the right response and stick it out to the bitter end. Sometimes it works and the person returns with renewed vigour; sometimes they need to go for good. Tunde and the team will always review what they did, so they can take the learning for next time.

Knowing you can manage challenge is of enormous value – you can't travel the life alignment curve without it – and it may be exactly the spur you need to move on to the next stage of development.

EXPLORATION

Look back at the previous exercise about significant learning experiences. Using the same examples, think about where the learning came from. For Harriet, the learning came from:

■ The teacher, Miss Lake, who told her not to be pleased with her first good mark, because she could have done better. Harriet took this as an encouraging comment about her ability and began to work harder.

■ The frustration of trying hard and still turning out poor work because of her dyslexia.

■ The challenge of proving herself in her degree and turning out a first class honours.

Now she knows what she can achieve and she knows where her limits are.

Write down your main learnings to see where they came from and what they taught you. Look for:

■ Common themes, so you can make good use of similar situations in the future.

■ Your preference: you will have a way of learning that works well for you, eg, some people work best with teachers, others are very good at analysing situations for themselves.

■ Where different types of learning come from so you know where to look for something specific.

Making the most of learning

Learning comes from all around us – but how do we make the most of it? The answer is to be conscious.

Some people glide through life without touching the sides, unconscious of personal impact. Experiences happen – activities come and go – but nothing changes. Responsibility is handed to anyone who will take it and inertia sets in. Continuing with such a lack of consciousness leads to a life unused, full of frustration and misery.

Serial achievers will have none of this – their aim is to take all the learning that life brings, putting it to good use as they grow and develop.

Being conscious requires you to develop the habit of regular review. This is familiar to those in business – checking to find out if the agreed targets/outcomes have been met is normal practice. Being a serial achiever means applying that same process to life itself, reflecting on all the elements of a day to identify what went well and what can be improved upon.

The habit of review

There are several ways to encourage such contemplation. First, find a way of tracking your learning that suits you. For some this is a journal; you may prefer to keep a record on your computer or mind map your way through the week. The method is only relevant to you, so choose the one you are most likely to stick to.

Second, don't put yourself under pressure to review things every day, unless you enjoy regularity and routine, in which case name your time and get going. If the idea of routine is a turn-off, then look for a way to remind yourself of the value of review, so you can choose the moments when you need to be conscious.

Third, think about events in your life that have taught you the most. If there is a theme, make sure you always use those times now to best effect.

Finally, identify the first event you will review and just start. On one hand, this is a 'non-essential' that you will want to put off until tomorrow. On the other, it is the one thing that can define your success – so go for it.

A starting point for conscious review looks something like Table 11.1.

Refine the questions to suit yourself and each situation. The intention is to look at the event from every angle to see what you learn and how you can take that learning forward into your next experience.

This process requires you to use deep honesty – anything else leads ultimately to unconsciousness and stagnation with only the 'best years of your life' to look back on.

Acquiring skills

Skills are appreciated and admired in our society, because they lead to a clear label:

- Andy Wraith is admired for being a doctor.
- Gina Coleman can be placed when she says she worked in public relations.
- People can relate to James Nathan once they know he is a chef.

We put people into categories by what they do and the skills they have. By acquiring a skill, you also get yourself a label, which makes life easier.

This is an interesting one for serial achievers. Their labels change as they travel through a number of life chapters, so people have to re-align their assumptions:

Table 11.1 Prompts for reviewing an event

	Going well and why	Not going well and why	Learning	Actions to be taken
Was I prepared for the event?				
Did I use my skills and core talent well?				
Did I communicate as I wanted to?				
What is the state of the relevant relationships?				
Did I have the effect I wanted?				
How well did I understand the situation?				
How honest was I with myself and with others?				
What did I do really well?				
What could I have done better?				

- People are amazed that Andy is also a dentist and an anaesthetist.
- Gina moves to a different box once people learn she is not paid for her work at the local hospice.
- Where do you place a chef who was a barrister?

Increasingly there is the expectation of ongoing change in career or work preference. However, the old tradition dies hard and it is tempting to look quickly for a skill so you know what to say when asked.

The question about skill comes to the fore as you reach the longed-for epiphany. Time in incubation can be frustrating, so any signs that you are through it and on your way to action are welcome. There will be a temptation to jump quickly, so stop for a moment to ask yourself the following questions:

- Am I focusing on my core talent? If not, it will be extremely hard to succeed.
- Do I really want to do it? Will it be exciting and challenging enough for me?
- Does it fit the direction of this life chapter?

"Am I focusing on my core talent?"

Finding the help you need

Once you know which way to go, then consider what help you need. Do you need to retrain or are you extending a skill you already have in embryo? There are options for each need:

- Retraining needs a course that takes you through the basics.
- Advancing a basic skill needs apprenticeship or mentoring.
- Adjusting direction requires coaching to help you refine your skill.

Attending courses

This is easy on one level because it puts all the training into one place and time. You know if you complete the course you will have the basics of the skill you need. Yet for many people it also carries with it mindsets about school, exams and fear of failure! So, remember you are not alone in this – many people will understand your anxiety. Also, as soon as you *choose* to learn something, your motivation is much stronger so it will be a different experience altogether. Finally, never be afraid to own up and find the help you need:

- go online and search for exam tips;
- ask the teacher for help or have some private tuition on exam technique;
- find someone in your network who has plenty of experience and pick their brains.

Above all, remember fear and dream has to collide – a little bit of healthy anxiety never hurt anyone and the day you pass will be one of the best!

Advancing a basic skill

If you have a skill that you want to take in a new direction, refine your ideas before seeking help, so you keep the uniqueness of your view. Then look for ways of learning more:

- find a mentor who has the knowledge you need and is willing to share it with you;
- ask for a secondment at work so you can try out the new area;
- find an 'apprenticeship' – work alongside someone who does the work you want;
- offer your skills to a voluntary organisation, making clear you are exploring something new;
- try out with friends – offer them your help for free, as a practice.

You also need to do this when you have completed a course. Training gives you the basics – life experience will make you an expert!

This is definitely the moment to ask for help – so don't be shy. Look at your network of contacts or ask around to find someone who knows.

Adjusting direction

You have the skills you need and want to use them in a different arena. You don't need someone to tell you – you already have the skill. What you need is someone to help you stretch your thinking and come up with new ways of utilising what you know so well.

Anyone who is good at asking questions and getting you to think will be of help – they don't need to know your work. This may be your backup person or a colleague in the same arena. Above all, keep questioning and reviewing to learn from every new situation.

You can also find an expert and get a bit of coaching help. I did this when beginning to give big presentations – help from an actress was invaluable in giving me some 'lift' when on stage. There are all sorts of experts out there, so use the web, ask about and follow up ideas as they arise.

Make yourself marketable

Eversley Felix sets out to make himself marketable and this is good advice for serial achievers. As you consider new skills, this is a useful measure – will it make you more marketable?

In his learning and development role, Eversley looks for trends as a clue to what will happen in the future. He then works out how he can position himself in the right place so he brings obvious benefit to his employer – because that is good for both of them.

Your market will be different from Eversley's, but the sentiment remains the same:

- keep an eye on your chosen arena and consider what you believe to be the future;

- get imaginative and see what interests you in that possible future – explore what would fit your core talent;

- follow your interest, develop your skills and build your network, so you are as marketable as you can be.

Where are you now?

Being conscious allows you to take learning from everyone you meet and every situation, so the wise serial achiever is always seeking the next challenge or bit of wisdom:

- You know to look at your personal gravity for positive 'lift' and inhibiting 'drag'.

- You will look for learning in very different places and know what suits you well.

- You will establish the all-important habit of reviewing your day or specific events, taking the learning this brings forward with you.

- You have an idea of where to go to look for the skills you need.

And then all you need to do is get focused . . .

BEHAVIOUR SEVEN

Get focused

SERIAL ACHIEVERS ARE ALWAYS FOCUSED – THEY KNOW WHERE TO CONCENTRATE THEIR EFFORTS

'I get incredibly intolerant of people who aren't prepared to work hard enough – I just want to get them off the project.' When he was twenty years old, Robin Millar managed to get a record deal, but there was no disc to show at the end of it, just the producer getting the sack. 'No one did a good job for me, so I like to help others overcome the odds.' And to do that he demands fully focused work from all the team.

It is not only in music that we need to focus on the job at hand. This is the only way to ensure that the watercolour of our dreams will ever become reality.

Dreaming and working are both fun in their own right, but much more productive together. Spend your life dreaming and you risk ending up frustrated. Working without a goal is demoralising when you have little to show at the end of the day.

Getting focused is an essential element of success, making sense of all the exploration and confusion of the incubation period. The delight of purposeful work is what drives serial achievers to bigger and better heights. After this experience, anything else pales into insignificance.

Working for what you want

Susan Bull opened her first shop in 1970. It was the days of Bus Stop and Biba – when everything was achievable if you were willing to work hard.

'I was frightened and excited. I had been working for a wholesale dress company, so I knew how the business worked. Jackie, my partner, knew the ledger and wages side, so we did the buying together and I did the merchandising.'

Jackie and Susan gave themselves a week to get up and running, to save paying rent when they weren't open. 'We worked all day, then rushed back to the shop to do the redecorating at night. The cash till was a drawer, we had a "ready reckoner adding machine" and all the labels were written by hand – it was real make do and mend. On our way back from buying, I would drive and Jackie would sit in the back, marking up the stock, so we could get it straight into the shop.'

The shop was a success and since then Susan has bought, run and sold a number of shops. Just as focused now when the time requires, she is fully committed to bringing interesting and 'delicious' fashion to her customers.

Focus and the life alignment curve

While the stages of the life alignment curve feel very different, they all need quality attention. Being focused either on your own development in the incubation period or on a new activity when driving forward will ensure you make the most of the opportunity for change and development.

Focus when restless

Restlessness is elusive and difficult to spot, so keep it in the back of your mind. Because it is so uncomfortable, the faster you pick it up, the sooner you can begin incubating your next move.

Experience frustration, boredom or loss of energy – anything that leaves you wanting to turn your back – and it is time to reflect on the cause. It may just be a sign that you have to move to the next stage in developing skills or style. It could also be signalling that a much bigger shift is imminent.

For a serial achiever, this is exciting as well as a bit daunting. You have done your best with your present life chapter and are feeling drawn towards a change. You feel unsure and might want to turn away, but the restlessness persists. Focus on what it is telling you and move on – life is about to get very interesting!

"Life is about to get very interesting!"

Focus during incubation

This time demands focus because, by its nature, incubation is a diffuse process. Having recognised you are no longer totally engaged in your present activity, you find yourself moving into a time of exploration. It can be anything from days to months before you gain any form of clarity about your next steps – so how on earth can you focus? The answer is to focus on the activities that will help you identify a goal, rather than bothering about the goal itself:

- Business as usual – you still have to eat!
- Getting the support you need.
- Paying attention to personal gravity.
- Building the first stages of your watercolour.
- Exploring all the options that come to mind.

Business as usual

Restlessness and incubation often strike at a time when you are apparently doing fine – work is going well, you are settled at home – yet something isn't right. You may not even know the cause of your dissatisfaction, so all you can do is sit with it for a while until the picture clears.

It's all very well to say 'sit with it', but the bills keep coming in, the car needs fuel and the fridge empties at a remarkable rate. So you have to keep going with your work – paid or otherwise – regardless of how you feel.

It is much easier to do this if you are clear what is happening – it allows you to put the experience into context:

- Working, while drowning in confusion, is hard-going – making it difficult to give your attention to the task at hand.
- Working, knowing that the confusion has a purpose and that this is you making your way through it, helps you relax into what is happening and frees up enough energy to keep going.

The only difference is putting understanding and context around the process – you are no longer just confused, you know you are confused and, daft as it sounds, that can make all the difference. Recognising the process means you also know:

- this is a time of growth and development;
- it will end and you will be better off;
- a new phase of your life is opening up.

None of which is nearly as bad as 'I feel dreadful and I have no idea what is happening or how to get out of it.'

So focus on delivering the work at hand. Do your job, look after the kids, meet your friends and allow yourself space for thought and relaxation when you need it.

Getting the support you need

As you enter a new phase of incubation, remember to keep your backup/support people informed – don't expect them to read your mind. Find time to take them through what is happening and use them as a sounding board for new ideas.

Remind them that you need to hear the truth – even when you least want to! If you don't encourage them, no one will speak until the level of frustration has risen so high that they can stand it no longer. And then you will have a lot more difficulty on your hands.

One very important point – if your backup people are also serial achievers, remember that they will be on their own life alignment curve. They will need backup too, so make sure you offer as well as receive.

Paying attention to personal gravity

Personal gravity will give you a lift into the next stage of development or drag you back mercilessly. Focusing attention on your own reactions will help you track which is happening, so you can deal with it in a timely manner.

EXPLORATION

Look back at the Second Fundamental to remind yourself of the different aspects of personal gravity. This is a great time to focus on your journal so you can explore what confuses, frustrates and angers you, and what makes you really animated and enthusiastic. Match these feelings against your mindsets, mottos, familiarity and life pressure and it will increase your self-knowledge substantially:

■ Lift:

- Notice when you feel excited and enthusiastic about changes brewing in your life. What sparks the feeling? What thoughts go with it? How does it lead you to act?

- Link those feelings to your personal gravity. What mindsets are activated? How do your mottos support you in moving forward?

- How can you use these positive drivers to help you further in
  incubation?

■ Drag:

- Write down when you feel bad tempered, deflated or fed up with
  having to manage change. How did you get into this state? What
  prompted your response?

- How does this link to your personal gravity. What mindsets, life
  pressures or familiarity have been sparked and what assumptions do
  they create?

- Think about the way these assumptions affect your next steps. How
  will they hold you back? Is this something you want? If not, what
  do you need to do right now to change that?

- Write down a clear statement of the assumption, then turn it to a
  positive and repeat that to yourself as you move through your day.

Personal gravity just feels like the norm. As long as the impact
is a positive one, use it to your advantage. When it is negative,
remember that this is just a bunch of behaviour patterns developed over time. You built them up, so you can take them down.
It may not be easy, but it is in your control. So take action as
soon as you can, and if you need help, ask for it.

Building the first stages of your watercolour

It is in incubation that the first glimmer of your vision for the
future will emerge. Remember that you don't need detail at this
point – in fact it will be detrimental – so let yourself enjoy the
hints and seed ideas as they appear.

Again, use your notebook liberally. Keep it with you at all times
and put it by the bed at night – you never know when a moment
of clarity is going to hit you. Write down any ideas that come to
mind – some will be useful and some will be pie in the sky, but
don't censor them – just write!

Part of the function of incubation is to take you into unknown territory, so inevitably you will come up with some thoughts and ideas that seem either high flown or too pedestrian to make any difference. However, they may be the precursor to something useful, so dismiss nothing. Give your full attention for as long as it makes sense – remember you are training your mind to look for opportunity (Behaviour Four).

Following your nose to success

While Tunde Banjoko was struggling to find his next step in life, he decided he would go into information technology, which was just beginning to take off. To fund it, he drove a mini-cab at night and went to college in the day.

'Then I saw an advert for someone to set up this little employment initiative – they wanted someone who knew about computers, so could set up a database; someone with sales experience and someone who knew about the issues of unemployment. I knew computers and was a good salesman plus I'd been out of work for two years, so, trust me, I knew all about unemployment! So I applied and got the job which was to set up what has become LEAP.

'I didn't intend to do it for very long. I only did it because it was a job that would tide me over until I got a highly paid computer job.

'We started in a small room and worked really, really hard to place people into work. Because we were located on the high street, when I went out for my lunch, I would see people we had helped. They would say, "Tunde – you got me this job – thanks very much." And I thought – this actually feels all right. I may not be making the money I wanted, but it actually feels good!'

Exploring options that come to mind

Tunde needed to follow his idea for working in computers because it led him to the work he loves in LEAP. In the same way, you won't always know what will lead you where, so all you can do is work with what is in front of you right now.

"All you can do is work with what is in front of you right now."

Naaz Coker learned a similar lesson from her university tutor Megan Blackmore: 'If you want to succeed or change, you have got to get on. Do something – don't just sit there waiting.' Naaz had applied to study dentistry, then discovered that she wasn't at all keen on saliva! However, the course led her to Megan who became like a second mother and helped her to relocate to pharmacy, which she really enjoyed.

Both Tunde and Naaz moved in the direction they thought was right, then found themselves moving to somewhere unexpected – but right! The same will be true for you:

- You may find the best choice straight away and settle into a positive life chapter.
- You may go in a direction that is OK and find it leads you to the right place.
- You may go in the wrong direction entirely but find that the lessons learned help you find your way to the right place.

Nothing is lost in life – even the most testing times teach you something. In fact, the testing times are often the most valuable – although it rarely feels like that at the time!

This view of success takes the pressure off finding the *right thing* to do with your life. Instead, you will go through a number of life chapters, some of which will be connected and some quite disparate. Go with what feels right at the time because:

- every activity will change you and your next step may need to be different as a result;
- as you mature, your needs change, so what you do now may not suit you in the future;
- life itself will change around you, opening up opportunities for you to use your core talent.

You don't need to know what to do in ten years' time, just what to do now. So take a step – knowing that you will learn and the learning will take you forward.

The epiphany

This is the most wonderful moment and deserves focus just for the delight of it! Finally, you can see the way forward. Like a honeymoon, it all looks obvious, simple and perfect. You are excited and bowled over by the possibilities.

James Nathan was faced with some tough decisions after his win on MasterChef – deciding on the right restaurant for him was a big epiphany. He was full of energy and thoroughly enjoyed the work that followed. Shortly after, came a second, minor epiphany as he saw what getting focused could do for him. He received a text from Michael Caines, a celebrated chef who had taken over the Priory restaurant, asking if he would join the new team. And only the day before he had been telling a friend how much he would love to work there! It was a wonderful moment and well deserved after all his hard work.

So enjoy your moment. Celebrate with friends and supporters and then write it all down in your journal. Next time you are in the doldrums you will need reminding that this moment *will* come round again.

Focusing on drive

As a result of your epiphany you will begin to drive forward. This requires you to manage yourself; plan the next steps; maintain focus.

Manage yourself

This is an exciting time. After being at sea, you are suddenly brimming with energy and pressing to move on. A bit like an arrow in a bow that has been held at full stretch for a long time – the slightest twitch of the fingers releases the string and you drive forward at full escape velocity.

While you are keen to use your energy, you also need to slow down long enough to get organised:

- Involve your backup and support people. Talk with them and share your excitement – they have been through the tough times with you, so let them revel in the upside too.

  Discuss your plan and explain the detail on your watercolour so they understand where it will take you. Not only will you benefit from getting them on board, it is also great practice in explaining your idea to another person – something you will certainly need to do again.

  The challenge at this point is to listen to a pessimistic response – you just want people to be excited! Remember they have your best interests at heart, so listen to the caring voices and act accordingly. Always take the comments into account – you don't have to act if you believe they are misguided, but never dismiss their views out of hand. You may find that paying attention to a small concern now will be invaluable in the long run.

  If you have any concern that your backup person is distracted and not able to hear what you have to say clearly, then have a conversation to explore what is going on. You may find that they are in a tough spot themselves – in which case, give them the support they need.

- Look at your mindset. Your epiphany may deliver up an idea that sits really comfortably, so you are absolutely ready to move on. In which case, off you go!

  However, it is also possible that you are facing something that is not only very exciting, but also rather daunting. In which case, it is useful to consider how your personal gravity may help or hold you back. Being prepared makes it much easier to spot the signs as they arise. So review your mindsets on success to make sure you are ready to go for it.

It is also really helpful to identity the thoughts and images that encourage you when demands or uncertainty is high:

- Andy Wraith recalls seeing people queue up for the soup kitchens in the miners' strike of 1984–85: 'It made me realise that I had to do it myself, that I had to be self-reliant.'

- For Gina Coleman, it was cleaning her grandfather's house on a Saturday morning. 'I liked the feel of the ten shilling note I got at the end of it. I am not motivated by lots and lots of money, but knowing there is something at the end seems to help me work harder.'

- Murray Dunlop has his vision of financial security and a happy, healthy family to keep him focused.

- James just knows he can endure. 'I bitch and moan, complain and fall apart, but I keep going, keep going, keep going. It sounds to other people as if I am giving up, but I am never broken. I just keep trudging on.'

Knowing what inspires you to greater action, even when the chips are down, will help when you feel as if you are getting nowhere. It needn't make sense to anyone else – as long as it makes sense to you.

"It needn't make sense to anyone else – as long as it makes sense to you."

Plan the next steps

You can work like mad and not get anywhere if you don't have a plan.

EXPLORATION

When your epiphany arrives, you have energy, determination and excitement. Moving into drive requires a plan of action so you get the best out of the enthusiasm available. First identify the style of planning that suits you, then consider the following:

- Outline the challenge: be clear about its different aspects – familiar and unfamiliar.

- Personal: what do you need to do to be ready? Personal presentation, CV up to date, family support and childcare, etc.

- Research: do you know the field well enough? What else do you need to know and where can you find it?

- Review: look to your network of contacts for someone with the knowledge you need, who will help you review your plan.

- Professional: support needed, eg, marketing, sales, web design, coaching, interview training.

- Training: any skills you need to develop before or on the job?

- Time: how will you manage your time to ensure you don't neglect other areas of your life?

- Financial: what are the implications of your plan and what action, if any, do you need to take?

Using your backup and support person or someone who has the specific understanding you need, go through the plan to identify gaps and areas for examination. Never be afraid to ask for help – the last thing you want is to waste any of that precious energy by going off down a blind alley.

Maintaining focus

With all the post-incubation energy flying around there are two risks:

- the excitement itself becomes a distraction and the temptation to talk about what you are doing overwhelms the actual doing;
- the energy takes over and work becomes overly dominant.

A lot of energy can be difficult to handle and requires some containment if anything is to be achieved. Serial achievers have to learn to enjoy the excitement and use it to celebrate the new focus and activity. They also need to channel the energy to where it can add value.

Getting focused pays off big time

Craig Fazzini-Jones set up his first business at the age of fifteen. The family were going through an extremely tough time financially, so he had to find a way to make any money he needed. A friend of his brother looked after gardens for cash-rich / time-poor people and Craig thought he would give it a go. It took just one advert and calls began coming in.

Weekly Weeders tended borders, built decking and mowed lawns, giving Craig the spending money he needed. Soon there was more work than he could handle alongside school, so he took on some of his friends to help. By putting them to work and taking a margin, he continued to make the most of the work stream he had created, putting aside money that would get him through college.

Craig realised early on that money didn't just show up, so he learned how to get focused. It has taken him to really exciting work in the banking and insurance sectors, making the most of that early business acumen.

Applying yourself will keep you motoring nicely in the drive stage of the life alignment curve. To achieve it you need to know the following about yourself:

- The real reason for doing the work – knowing this underlines the importance of focus.

- How you distract yourself – be specific about what you do as a way of avoiding the task.

- The risk – or perceived risk – of being really focused, ie, what scares you about achieving your goals – logical or otherwise?

- The impact of not delivering in the agreed time frame – does this matter to you? If so, why?

- How you will feel about yourself at the end of the day if you haven't done what you set out to do? Be very specific about this. Define exactly why you don't want to be there!

When work is new and unfamiliar it is easy to take longer over a task – at least then for a short time you know what you are doing! As soon as you start to go for it, there is a chance you will make a mistake or get it wrong and that is a little scary.

I recall writing a course for a business client with a colleague. It was a really exciting programme that would open up a lot of opportunity. It was also very new and we were both on unfamiliar territory. We talked it through together, allocated tasks and then went to separate rooms to each write a specific element. As I blundered around trying to work out how to begin, I heard a voice call from the kitchen: 'Judith, the fridge needs cleaning. Will you do it or shall I?'

Challenging work can suddenly make washing, cleaning, dog walking or shopping seem remarkably appealing. You can give in to it or you can make yourself focus. Times like this call for a real act of will – being determined that you will complete what you set out to complete whatever happens. Do it once and it will be easier next time.

"Challenging work can make washing, cleaning and dog walking remarkably appealing."

This is always important to serial achievers, since the process of going from one peak to another regularly calls you into new areas and open water. Part of the excitement is the novelty, so learning how to make the most of it is essential.

Focus on enjoying stability

Now you really know what you are doing and focus becomes easier, demanding less of you. However, that also makes it tempting to coast, which will in time become boring, so:

- set yourself clear goals and make sure they provide a stretch that feels worthwhile and interesting;

- make this a time of real learning – keep your review times thorough and honest. This will give you a head start into your next life chapter;

- ask for feedback from those who work with you and support you. They will help you stay focused on delivering top quality;

- look around for people you can support and help – pay back some of the support you received when in need or pay forward for next time;

- devote time to your network, including new people who are relevant to this life chapter.

Maintaining focus on your learning and attitude during this time will make the next round of the life alignment curve easier. Growing and maturing with each peak will ensure you have more skill, ability and refinement to take with you – which in turn will make the whole process more slick and smooth.

The downside of getting focused

Focus, by its nature, is totally absorbing. It is easy to go on for hours with no idea how much time has passed. Starting a new area of work really does require consistent focus as you work to find a foothold, but if the time period is too protracted or no break is taken, then stress can be the result. And if a pattern of constant work and long hours takes over, then it is easy to lose touch with the very people who could point out what is happening.

Once a life chapter is nearing the end, normality starts to rock a little and it is tempting to home in on the familiar, in order to re-assert control. But this focus drains energy because the passion has gone. There is no fault in this, but it does require the person to employ some deep honesty and begin to embrace the change. Once they do this, their enthusiasm will start to return – even if it is a bit scary!

Any sign of stress needs attention but you may not notice it yourself. This is one very good reason for listening to backup and support people – they will probably see it long before you do.

Always pay attention when you can't sleep, lack focus or interest, feel ill or can't be bothered with life. As ever, first port of call – take a health check. If that is OK, then you may well be at the point of restlessness, ready for a change and crying out for attention!

Enjoy your success – then let it go

Success is wonderful – something to be enjoyed and celebrated. It is really satisfying to be doing the right thing:

- your energy will soar and you will achieve more than you ever thought possible;

- outputs will be really worthwhile and people will appreciate what you have to offer;
- you will be at your most creative, coming up with ideas and thoughts for how to improve;
- your enthusiasm will be contagious and family and friends will enjoy being with you;
- you will be learning, both for now and for the future.

"Success is wonderful – something to be enjoyed and celebrated."

Because this time is so good, it is tempting to try and hold on. But do that for too long and the taste will begin to sour.

Success is about knowing that you have used your core talent well. But core talent has so much potential it won't rest until stretched and challenged again. As a serial achiever, this is just one peak. As soon as this one is done, a new one will start to brew. And each one will be bigger and better than the one before.

So enjoy now and, as soon as the time is right, let go and begin your next life alignment curve, taking the learning from this one with you.

As you take up and complete each life chapter, you will learn, grow and mature. And when you sit in your chair at ninety years old, you will look back and say, 'This has truly been a life well used!'

Index

Hear more from Judith Leary-Joyce...

'Inspirational Manager'

Some bosses are better than good – they're inspirational. Their teams deliver exceptional performance because they can't imagine letting their manager down. These inspirational managers earn more respect, suffer less stress and produce better results than other managers. Want to be one? This book tells you how.

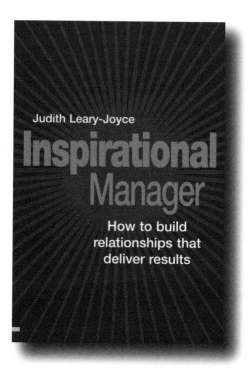

Judith Leary-Joyce

Inspirational
Manager

How to build
relationships that
deliver results

Drawing on the experiences of real inspirational managers, facing real challenges and managing real people, *Inspirational Manager* gives you the tools and techniques to ensure that people notice you and say – "Now there's a great manager!"